Finally Free

Breaking free from the cycle of abuse
and finding emotional healing

ORTAVIA TAYLOR

Finally Free

Breaking free from the cycle of abuse
and finding emotional healing

ORTAVIA TAYLOR

T&J PUBLISHERS

A SMALL INDEPENDENT PUBLISHER WITH A BIG VOICE

Printed in the United States of America by
T&J Publishers (Atlanta, GA.)
www.TandJPublishers.com

© Copyright 2019 by Ortavia Taylor

All rights reserved. This book or parts thereof may not be reproduced in any form, stored in a retrieval system, or transmitted in any form by any means-electronic, mechanical, photocopy, recording, or otherwise-without prior written permission of the author, except as provided by United States of America copyright law.

All Scriptures used are from the King James Version Bible (KJV), the New Living Translation (NLT), and the New International Version (NIV)

Cover Design by Timothy Flemming, Jr. (T&J Publishers)
Book Format/Layout by Timothy Flemming, Jr.
Photography by Tara Harp Photography (taraharpphotos@gmail.com)

ISBN: 978-1-7335470-6-2

To contact author, go to:

www.JustTaylorMade.com
Justtaylormade1@gmail.com
Instagram: JustTaylorMade1
Facebook: Just Taylor Made

Business Contact Number:
(678) 671-1615

DEDICATIONS

I dedicate this book to my three beautiful daughters, Ashley, Deshantia, and Raynesha. You are one of the reasons for me walking in freedom and total deliverance. My prayer for you is that, as you read this book, it will give you clarity and peace in your heart, mind, and soul. Hopefully, you'll begin to understand why I made some of the choices I did concerning you—why I was so protective of you, the tough love I showed you, and the pressure I put on you to become strong women who could stand up for yourselves. You are all beautiful and intelligent. Be all that God has called you to be. Like I always said to you, for every choice you make, there is a reality of consequences waiting in the shadows, yearning to convince you to do wrong or convict you to do what's right.

Being a single mother in my situation took bravery. Lord knows it was no easy task. I had to be a rock and a shield. My inner voice reminded me daily that the Lord was ordering my steps, and God chose my life to be a testimony of survival. Through all the bits and pieces, and even when I felt like giving up, God kept me. That's the legacy I want to leave with you, a legacy of faith. When fear bound me and I felt broken, God restored my soul. He gave me the strength to get up and move when I was too weak to keep going. He kept me in that valley experience. When I was living foolishly, I had no clue that the decisions I was making would one day become a thorn in my side, but God set me free from my shame and my past and He took what was originally meant to destroy me and used it to bless me. When I look back over my life, all I can say is "Thank you, Lord, that I'm finally free to share my story."

I'm on a new path in life, but I'll never stop being mom. Nothing will change "the mother" in me. It's my job to protect you and encourage you to do the right thing. You've witnessed the things I endured, and you saw my example, now heed the signs and avoid making the same mistakes in your lives.

Although I made many mistakes, today I have the victory; and to be honest, I can't say I would change a thing. I am not ashamed of my testimony, nor am I a prisoner of my past; and even though I'm not perfect, I'm certainly not the woman I used to be. The only *pinch* is considering that the woman you looked to as your hero was silently being beaten and stripped of her character, and out of fear nearly lost my faith and myself even while attempting to shield you from what was happening.

As I write, tears fill my eyes. I was just lost, broken, and confused; and although I knew intuitively that love isn't supposed to hurt, I mistakenly chose to do nothing about it. I am sorry that you had to experience such things in our home, and I pray that this book brings guidance, closure, and healing to your hearts. I also pray you'll forgive me if I have failed you in any way. Most of all, I assure you, this will never happen again.

Love you endlessly,
Your Mother

ACKNOWLEDGMENTS

I give all thanks to my Heavenly Father whom has filled me with every spiritual blessing. Many times, it seemed you were so far away, but I learned that at my weakest point you were carrying me. You never took your hand off me. I owe you my life; and as long as I live, I will tell of your goodness through my story. Your agape love has taken me from bitter to better, broken to being whole, from victim to victorious, and un-forgiven to being able to truly forgive.

To my life coach, Niya Brown Matthews, thanks for your consistently pushing me and holding me accountable to complete whatever I start.

To Tara Evans, thank you so much for your obedience to our Heavenly Father concerning me. At a low place in my life you came and pulled me out of lode bar.

To my personal Blacque Michelangelo, you know who you are. Thank you for your unwavering support during the time I needed it the most. The journey was not easy, but I am truly grateful for your truth and the eagerness to see me succeed in my future endeavors. Even when it got heated, you remained the same. You worked unselfishly behind the scenes. You worked diligently, and I am forever grateful. Thank you so much

Lastly, Jeromiah, it is because of you I can, and will, be my best me. Your love is never failing, and you always push me when I don't want to be pushed. The excitement you possess in knowing the outcome is priceless.

To everyone I didn't name, special thanks to you for all your support. I love you.

The key to changing
from Victim to Victorious is
Forgiveness.

Table of Contents

Foreword	xiii
Introduction: It's Always Pretty In The Beginning	15
Chapter 1: Damaged	21
Chapter 2: The Things We Choose To Ignore	31
Chapter 3: The First Hit	41
Chapter 4: My Time In Prison	49
Chapter 5: A New Low	59
Chapter 6: Everybody Plays The Fool	71
Chapter 7: The Devil Always Comes Back	83
Chapter 8: Out Of Control	93
Chapter 9: Free At Last	107
The Final Word	129

FOREWORD
by Crystal Pugh Boyd and Niya Brown Matthews

Dr. Crystal Pugh-Boyd,
CEO of Crystal Pugh Ministries

One of the hidden mysteries of humankind is discovering the full potential of your freedom in life. A lack of freedom is the reason why people behave in ways that are outside of the realm of God's purpose for their lives.

This book "Finally Free" will help you to strategically unleash the God-given freedom that will thrust you into your destiny. You will become equipped in discovering your freedom from what once had you bound and what seemed to have unbreakable chains [on you]. No matter what the situation you are facing and have faced from your past, you will realize that God has ordained greater for your life.

Ortavia Taylor, a victim of domestic abuse herself, has written this gut-wrenching powerful book that will unlock you out of abusive strongholds that you have been chained to due to fear and satanic control.

This masterpiece of truth and boldness will empower you to take control of your life and your God-given strength. You will take back your power and your true identity. You will be thrust into the freedom of empowerment, strength, and live in God's abundant blessings.

Ortavia Taylor is a woman of God in whom I am proud to endorse.

Get this book and read it more than once so you can

soak every hidden mystery within it. Get a copy for a friend and loved one. With Love and Many Blessings!

Niya Brown Matthews,
Certified Life Coach. Author. Motivational Speaker
(Soulfoodsessionswithniya.com)

Ortavia Taylor story is one that is so needed in a time such as this. Many people have been suffering in silence not knowing where to turn or how to be set free. Meeting Ortavia and then having a life coaching session with her I was in awe of hearing her story of life. Her testimony will truly give one hope. As a Certified Life Coach often times I see people can't be see free because they are not willing to face this issues, the pain, the hurt. This holds them bound from being whole. Ortavia was willing to stare her past hurts in the face and knock them down like a bull dozer. She decided she was no longer going to be held back from her destiny, her purpose. That takes great courage. We all know it will be a daily walk, or climb to up the hill of Destiny but Ortavia's perseverance and dedication as well as faith will help carry her to the mountaintop. Being an Author myself, writing is a great tool used to help cope and process life. I believe sharing one's testimony or story can not only see you free but help set many free. I'm ecstatic Ortavia has made the decision to turn her pain into purpose and sharing her story will indeed set many people free and give them hope after they read her book.

INTRODUCTION

IT'S ALWAYS PRETTY IN THE BEGINNING

> Okay. I'm done. That was the final straw. This man just shot up my house, trying to kill me! I got to get out of here! If I don't make it out of here, I'm going to turn up dead somewhere. Things have gotten that crazy. But he seemed like such a nice guy at first. How in the world did I end up in this situation?

AT SOME POINT, EVERY ABUSE VICTIM STOPS AND asks themselves that question: *How did I end up in this situation?* They ask themselves that because they never intended to end up in an abusive situation. No one wakes up in the morning and says, "Hey, I want to get hit, slapped, punched, kicked, stomped, and abused in every way imaginable! It'll be fun!" None of us want to be treated that way; and yet, this is the reality billions of people have to endure daily. Regular, ordinary people just looking for love and companionship get caught in the trap of abusive relationships, suffering cruel and inhumane treatment by people they thought would love them, people they decided to trust; and for many, after being abused for so many years, they've begun to accept it as a way of life. They've stopped dreaming and looking for something better, and have believed the lie that claims there's no way out, and this is how it's going to be always; they've even begun telling themselves they deserve to be treated this way. None of this is true, but this is what they believe.

I found myself in that same spot several years ago. Whether he was trying to scare me or not, my ex-boyfriend did fire several shots into my house while outside, and that's when I realized how much danger I was in. It's as if I'd suddenly awaken from a dream and discovered how much of a nightmare I was living in. At that moment, I realized this was not a game; it wasn't going to end unless I was dead. I had too much to live for, too much to do in this world, children that depended on me, family members that loved me, and a purpose to fulfill in this world. I didn't have time to delude myself with lies anymore to justify my situation. I had to wake up and face reality. For had I not awaken when I did, I wouldn't be writing this book today.

As I stated earlier, no one plans to be abused; and by the way, it doesn't "just happen." It is something that gradually becomes a norm as we relinquish more control while giving more power over our lives to someone else. We begin to relinquish control over our lives once we fall for specific lies that make us feel unworthy, not good enough, and pow-

Introduction: It's Always Pretty...Beginning

erless; and don't worry, throughout this book, I'll pinpoint these lies so that you can remove them from your life. If you recognize any of these lies and discover that they're the ones you tell yourself, then it is crucial that you stop telling yourself these things and begin to speak the opposite. Again, don't worry because I'm also going to lead you into the things you need to say to yourself. You see, once I began telling myself the truth, I was able to walk away from a toxic relationship even after I'd invested much time into it. It was simple. When I learned the truth, I was done with accepting something that was not a part of God's plan for my life. It was quite easy to walk away. However, you have to know the truth about who you are and what God predestined for you to have in life.

For me, the abuse didn't "just start." It was a gradual process leading up to me being slapped, punched, kicked, thrown around, and more. It was a gradual process of me giving up the fight and accepting the abuse. It took a little time for my abuser to grow comfortable with treating me the way he did. In the beginning, he knew he had to put on his best face; he had to put on a good act. You see, these scenarios usually start like a dream come true, but then they quickly evolve into a nightmare; and truth be told, you can't merely spot an abuser by looking at a person's outer appearance. Many abusers will start out like a prince charming or a little princess. They don't come with the scarlet letter "A" plastered across their chests ("A" for "abuser"). They don't have red leathery looking skin, horns, and carry pitchforks. Most abusers look and act like normal, ordinary, mentally, and emotionally healthy people, but this is all an act to cover up their dark sides. Also, it doesn't matter what field or profession they're in; an abuser may be a professional such as a lawyer, doctor, even a judge or police officer. They may also be religious figures. *We often forget that Satan comes as an angel of light.* The point being, looks can be deceiving. It's not that the abuser is an evil person; don't get that idea in your head. Some abusive people just don't know any better. They haven't been taught the proper way to handle conflict. They may have seen abuse modeled before them in their lives, and that's how they think things get done. Furthermore, abuse is based on the desire to control others. When seeking control over others, these people will use physical violence, intimidation, and manipulation against them; this reveals another problem, which is that the abuser him or herself is suffering from a sickness and needs help ... but you're not the one to give it to them. That's the job of a professional. They have to want to get well. Your job, however, is to stay alive, to keep safe, and protect your family from harm and danger.

One thing that will reveal the truth about a person is time. It gets exhausting after a while to maintain a facade. So if you give it enough time, they will slip up and do something or say something that indicates their true nature and intentions. It's vital that the second you see the truth about the person you're with you make the wise decision to avoid entangling yourself into their web of deception. Remember, Proverbs 22:24-25 says,

> "Don't befriend angry people or associate with hot-tempered people, or you will learn to be like them and endanger your soul." (NLT)

Sounds pretty clear. Be careful that you don't fall into the

Inroduction: It's Always Pretty...Beginning

trap of thinking you can change a person who's already angry, hateful and bitter in life. That person has to allow God to do the work of transformation in their life, which means they have to be more accountable to God than to you. You don't have the power to change anyone else, and thinking you do will only set you up for a trap. That's why you have to pray and trust God to send you your mate, and you have to observe that person's walk with God. As Paul tells us,

> "Don't team up with those who are unbelievers. How can righteousness be a partner with wickedness? How can light live with darkness?" (2 Corinthians 6:14, NLT)

If that person doesn't have a relationship with God, that's a sign. If that person doesn't live in accordance with God's Word, that's a sign. If that person doesn't fear God, that's a sign. If that person doesn't care about the state of his or her soul, that's a sign. If that person's primary concern is pleasing you or themselves over pleasing God, that's a sign. *A sign of what?* That you're walking into trouble. Forget about the horoscopes; these are the real signs to look for.

Don't be fooled by smiles, cuteness, kind words, flattery, and beautiful gifts. These are the pretty beginnings many people fall for, the smokescreens that make many people feel as if they're walking into a good thing; but I'm going to show you how to avoid that pitfall and make wise decisions when it comes to choosing a partner—if that's what you are looking to do. If not, that's fine also. Either way, I'm going to show you how to find freedom from abuse, recover your life, and be who you were created to be so that you can

Finally Free

stand up, as I did, and finally shout at the top of your lungs, "I'M FINALLY FREE!"

CHAPTER 1

DAMAGED

Usually, whenever we see a woman, for example, living with an abusive partner, we automatically assume she must have grown up in an abusive household where she witnessed physical violence and even experienced it. It's hard for us to imagine someone living that way after being raised in a loving, healthy, and safe environment. The victim must have seen his or her father beat their spouse. They had to have been exposed to this type of activity for them to view abuse as acceptable, as a norm, or misidentify it as an expression of love; but I'm here to tell you that's not always the case. You can come out of a good household and still become a victim of abuse.

Repeated abuse can take a toll on your mind if you don't escape it early. Many abuse victims start out with high expectations, but they allow their expectations to be reduced to rubble over time. They're then made to believe their standards are unrealistic, and then they're broken down systematically in order to accept sub-human standards. When you think about the slaves that were brought here from Africa, many of them were used to being free. They walked around free, spoke freely, ate and lived freely. Sadly, however, over a period of time and through a series of dehumanizing abuses suffered at the hands of their captors, they began to accept slavery as their ultimate fate and even think like slaves; this is the same thing that happens to many abuse victims today: they go from being independent to being systematically dependent, from having dignity to being degraded.

That's how it happened for me. That's my story.

Becoming a victim is about losing yourself; it's about what you choose to believe about yourself and what demons you decide to ignore. I'd created demons in my own life that I refused to deal with, and that is what set my feet upon the path to becoming a victim of domestic abuse. It was the choices I made and the lies I told myself.

MY CHILDHOOD

I was one of nine children growing up in a cramped house. Our little house squeezed twenty-four people inside of it. My mom was a hard-working woman who did her best to take care of all of her children. My dad was around, although he and my mom never married. He and mom had seven kids together—I was the oldest out of those seven kids. Dad decided instead to marry another woman and start a separate family; that decision increased the pressure that was already bearing down on our struggling household.

We grew up poor, and we knew it. The only times my siblings and I received anything new were on Christmas and

Chapter 1: Damaged

Easter holidays. We were used to hand-me-downs since we really couldn't afford new clothes.

Witnessing so much struggle while young birthed inside of me an enterprising spirit; it produced within me a strong desire to live a better life. I became a little entrepreneur, a little workaholic. I'd get up early and help pick beans with my great uncle on weekends, I'd babysit other days, and I'd help my grandmother clean houses, which she did for a living. I'd become determined not to live poor for the rest of my life. I became Little Ms. Independent.

I didn't witness my mom and dad engage in physically abusive behavior towards each other. Sure, they argued like most couples, but that was where the line was drawn. I didn't have an abusive father. My dad loved his children and continued to be in our lives. My grandpa and grandma were also prominent figures in our lives. I'd see them argue and fuss. Also, grandpa liked to drink, but he and grandma were certainly no *Ike and Tina*. Our household wasn't plagued by physical violence, although it was far from perfect. Hand-to-mouth living was our main issue, and it was stressful.

When I turned eleven-years-old, that's when things took a turn for the worst for us. That's when my dad passed away. After his death, we relocated from our little house to a drug-infested, crime-ridden neighborhood, which only added to the pressure we were already experiencing.

When I was finally old enough to leave the house, I left. I was excited to leave; probably too excited. I was more excited about what I was leaving behind than what I was running into. I had an "I got to get out of this place by any means necessary" attitude. My quest for a better life drove me to do something I knew was foolish. I began dating one

Finally Free

of the biggest drug dealers in town.

I was a ride-or-die chic. I had that man's back. I was willing to walk through the fire with him, and I did. Whenever his life was threatened, mine was too. If he got busted, I was also looked upon as a suspect. Sure, there were perks in the streets, but there were far more risks involved. It was nice being able to buy the things I wanted but never could afford when living at home with my mom and siblings. It felt great being able to eat in restaurants I could only imagine eating in previously. But as the old saying goes: *When it rains, it pours.* When the storm came, it hit hard.

All of the luxury and pampering came to an end when my boyfriend got arrested and sent off to prison for several years. At that point, I was left alone to take care of myself. Still, I had decided to wait for him. Again, I was loyal. I was also naive in thinking he was completely faithful to me and me alone. It's hard to see yourself as part of a harem, especially when you're continually being told that you're the *only* one. *Yeah, right.*

My heart was busted open the day that my boyfriend betrayed me while locked up. I was thinking that when he got out, I was going to be his woman. I was prepared to receive him again and embrace him as my man. We were going to rebuild together and create a life and a family together. I was mistaken. He ended up marrying another woman while still behind bars. I was devastated. I couldn't believe it. *How could he do this to me after all I put up with from him?* I thought to myself.

That man moved on with his life as if I didn't even exist, and that left a big hole in my heart. Anger took hold of me and I decided to get even rather than get healed. So I

Chapter 1: Damaged

chose to rebound with another man out of revenge.

The Rebound

I found a new man. He was tall, handsome, and a drug dealer. Of course, his lifestyle didn't bother me. To me, it was just life. All around me people hustled. They hustled to eat. They hustled to make ends meet. Bright, intelligent, and smart, they decided to apply their business acumen to a dangerous field. *Street pharmacists.* That's what some people call them. That's how I saw it. I didn't care how he made his money; all I cared about was how he treated me. If he could supply the demanding lifestyle I wanted, I was fine. I wanted the good life, something that would be a far cry from the poverty I'd grown up in; and, of course, just a little bit of revenge on the guy that left me for another woman.

There I was, moving ahead without knowing where I was going and what I was doing. First, I was running from poverty, now I was chasing after revenge. I was simply reacting to life's circumstances rather than getting a handle on my life. That was a big mistake. I needed to slow down and get my mind right, my heart healed, and discover God's plan for my life, but I felt I didn't have the time for all of that. I never had a vision or a plan. I was just running and reacting. The Bible says in Proverbs 29:18,

"Where there is no vision, the people perish."

Perish here means "to lose restraint; to be loosed." So, their minds are all over the place. They don't know who they are, what they should be doing, who and what to look for in life. Their emotions and their circumstances rule them. I like the

Finally Free

New Living Translation of this verse. It words it this way:

> "When people do not accept divine guidance, they run wild."

I was wilding out. I was living based on my emotions, jumping from one man to the next. I lacked wisdom and *divine* guidance; it's not like I was seeking God for His will for my life. I was doing what I wanted to. The more I lived this way, the more damage I did to my own heart by placing myself in precarious positions. I'd first get hurt and then look for a new relationship to medicate the pain. I never took the time to get myself together and get focused on the right things.

This new guy and I had a good relationship, at least, in the beginning. He did his thing in the streets, but never came home and abused or mistreat me in any way. He treated me good. We eventually got married. Again, everything was good ... in the beginning. We got along well and enjoyed being together. We did plenty of things as a couple. We had a child together before getting married, and I already had two children from the previous relationship, so we'd become one big happy family. Things were going great; but as time progressed, things began to go downhill.

You may have heard that there are different forms of abuse. This is true, and I was about to experience one of them. No, it wasn't physical abuse—thank God my husband didn't beat me. Also, it wasn't emotional abuse. My husband didn't go out of his way to demean me or make me feel small; he didn't try to reduce my self-esteem to ashes so that I'd feel ugly and undesirable. He didn't step on my dreams or do anything like that. However, the type of abuse I began to

Chapter 1: Damaged

suffer was neglect. To neglect someone or something means "to fail to take proper care of; to disregard." When parents do this to their children, DEFACs is called in, and the child is taken into custody, and then they are relocated to a safe environment. Even a pet that gets neglected by its owner is confiscated by The Humane Society and taken to a safe environment where it can thrive. Negligence is destructive to marriages and relationships. Whatever you ignore and disregard will fall into a state of ruin. The same is to be said about the heart. Neglected spouses usually suffer in silence for many days, weeks, months, even years, dealing with their frustrations, hidden pains, and pent up tension, which can place a lot of stress on their heart and put them in the grave.

I know God doesn't intend for us to get stuck in loveless, affection-less, dead relationships. He doesn't intend for our hearts to be neglected and cast aside while our needs go unmet. That's why He's so hellbent on healing broken hearts, and He's always telling us to cast our cares at His feet (1 Peter 5:7). The Bible tells us a "hope deferred makes the heart sick" (Proverbs 13:12). Therefore, when we desperately long for something but fail to get what we desire, we begin to feel sick inside; our hearts become ill. I believe this is the source of many of the sicknesses we experience in our bodies. I believe this is a major source of depression in the lives of many people—their hopes and dreams have been deferred (unfulfilled).

As time passed, I began to feel sick internally. I wanted my husband to love me, show me attention, and take care of the basic things around the house, but he abandoned his responsibilities to focus on other things. He forgot about *us*. While he was in *the trap*, I felt trapped in a loveless marriage. It didn't matter how much I communicated with him how I felt; we continued to drift apart. We became strangers living under one roof; this began to eat me alive inside. I so desperately wanted someone that I could connect with on an emotional, mental, and physical level; someone who'd be responsible, someone who'd attend to the needs of the home rather than putting me in the position to do everything myself, someone that would fill the void in my soul. Instead of getting that, all I received was the feeling of rejection while standing in the cold of abandonment. Basically, it was like I was single; but I was married, and that's what made things a lot more complicated. When you're single, your actions hold no legal recourse. Come and go if and when you please, but that isn't the case with marriage.

I was emotionally damaged. My heart was devastated by my previous boyfriend who I thought I would spend the rest of my life with; and now, my three-year marriage with a man I'd come to love—I say that because, in the beginning, I didn't love my husband, not the way I should have—was on the rocks. There was so much going on I didn't know where to turn and what to do.

I was a mess. I never took the time to get healed emotionally from all of the pain I suffered. Time doesn't heal all wounds as some people claim; actually, it does the opposite; it can harden our hearts and blind us to the wounds festering in our souls. If you don't treat gangrene in time, catching it early rather than ignoring it and letting it linger, it will spread throughout your body and eat away at you, even damaging major organs; eventually, it will cause an infection that will lead to death. Likewise, you don't ignore a heartbreak, thinking it will just disappear. You have to treat

Chapter 1: Damaged

it. You have to get healed from it so that it won't fester and ooze with a puss, becoming infected, and damage your soul.

Why is this important to mention? It's because sick people prey on sick people. When you're not well emotionally, you become an easy target for those who don't mean you well. Abusers look for people that are emotionally weak and vulnerable, who are emotionally wounded, who are desperate for love and acceptance—people who, like me, have been damaged. Being damaged is what opened a door in my life for the next man, the one that forever changed my life.

Points To Remember

- Never look for your identity and self-worth in a relationship. Take the time to discover these things before jumping into a relationship.
- Looking for a "rebound" relationship when hurt will only further damage your heart and distract you from getting healed emotionally and rebuilding your self-esteem.
- Possessing low self-esteem increases your chances of becoming a victim of domestic violence. Remember: It doesn't matter if you don't come from a broken home; what matters is that you are "broken" self-image and a broken sense of confidence.

CHAPTER 2
THE THINGS WE CHOOSE TO IGNORE

I WAS DAMAGED BUT PROUD. I WANTED TO COME ACROSS to others as having it all together even though I was suffocating inside. I didn't want to appear hurt and desperate, although I was hurt and desperate. My husband and I were estranged from one another, we were still living like strangers. Our marriage was already over. We were simply counting down the days until the inevitable divorce. I was looking for ways to blow off some steam. I was determined not to sit around the house with the shades drawn, moping in the dark. I wanted to get out and do something to take my mind off of things; go somewhere with someone. I wanted and needed to spend time with family and friends. I was excited when I was asked to attend a get-together with family and friends that was out of town, which was even better. I attended the event, looking my cutest. While there, I ended up catching the eye of a guy who apparently didn't know the meaning of the word "no."

THE FLING

This guy, who I wasn't interested in, just kept trying his best to flirt with me; and to make matters worse, we were on an elevator together, so there was no escape. Maybe it was the boos or a mental handicap, but he just wouldn't back off. It's like he didn't understand the meaning of the words "I'm not interested" and "Will you please leave me alone." He was like the Terminator—he just kept coming, flirting, and invading my space. He was like a thorn in my side.

He wasn't letting up despite my best attempts to get him off of me. The subtle attempts to touch me kept coming. If I had some mace, I probably would have emptied the whole thing in his face. Fortunate for him, I didn't have any; but thankfully, someone came to my rescue after sensing my distress. Hallelujah!

We'll call him Mike. There Mike was, towering like a tall, brave prince over the little troll that was annoying me. He confronted the bug-a-boo—who also happened to be his friend—and made him back off of me while on that elevator.

Mike was tall, handsome, well-mannered, and pretty easygoing. I felt an instant attraction to him, although I continued to play it cool. We clicked and hit it off. That night, we had a one-night stand. Lord knows I was more than ready to blow off some steam. Afterward, we exchanged contact information and went our separate way.

Despite sleeping together, I was in no hurry to get in a serious relationship. I just wanted that night to be a fling,

Chapter 2: The Things We Choose To Ignore

something that just happened without any strings attached. I wanted to maintain my sense of independence. Mike didn't seem troubled by that. Mike understood that; after all, I told him that I was in the middle of a divorce proceeding. At the time, I was still living in the same house with my soon-to-be ex-husband. We were like strangers, though, sleeping in separate rooms. I had decided when I got home to move out of that house and get my own place. So I found a two bedroom apartment and eventually moved out.

Shortly after I got my own place, Mike stopped by to visit, which was a pleasant surprise. He began coming by more often and we started spending more time together. I didn't consider the two of us as being in a serious relationship, however. I only saw us as *friends with benefits*. No commitments. No expectations. It was all about sex, booty-calls. That's all I wanted, but that didn't last long. It wouldn't take long before Mike ended up moving in with me, and our fling would develop into a full-fledged relationship.

At first, Mike was like a dream come true. He had it going on in the "looks department"; but what impressed me more was the fact that he took an immediate interest in my girls. He became a mentor to them, giving them great advice on life and sports. He was heavily involved with them, being a disciplinarian with a gentleness—not fussing, but lovingly talking to the girls. Everything my husband wasn't, Mike appeared to be. He seemed to be more family oriented. *Ahhh! A breath of fresh air!* We enjoyed our time together, going to family reunions, the movies, bowling, and more. We started to look and feel like a real family.

Even though I had always been a working girl, I believed in having a man that had no problem with taking the

Finally Free

leadership role in the household. I wanted a man that would work and spend his money on his family, and not just himself. I didn't mind working. I certainly didn't have a problem with contributing to the household, but I didn't want to be the one that got out and worked only to come home to a lazy man that acted like a kid, wanting me to pay all the bills, cook dinner, see to the kids, and then satisfy his sexual needs before going to bed. I wanted a man in the traditional sense: strong, responsible, dependable, decisive, confident; a leader. With Mike, that's what I'd hoped I was getting. Time would tell.

Mike seemed to have a good heart. He was supportive of my goals, cheering me on to pursue them, encouraging me to focus on school. He couldn't have been more perfect. Truthfully, he seemed just a little too perfect. And as you've probably suspected, it wasn't long before that perfect facade started to wear off and I began noticing a few red flags that screamed "DANGER!!"

RED FLAGS

Mike had many good qualities as I stated a moment ago. He seemed like a great catch. However, there were some things that stood out about him that troubled me, things that began to manifest themselves over time. It didn't take long for these character flaws to reveal themselves either; it just took enough time for Mike to get relaxed and let down his guard.

The first warning sign (or red flag) came when, shortly after I got my apartment, I received a phone call from Mike. Now, when he called me, it was around 5 am. Again, this was at the beginning of our fling stage before Mike moved in. I didn't think anything of it at the time. I just waived it off

Chapter 2: The Things We Choose To Ignore

as if what he did was harmless, and even cute. He called to inform me that he saw my husband leave out of my apartment. I didn't think about it then, but looking back today, I know now that he was stalking me. I should have asked *Why are you in front of my house at five in the morning, anyway? Or better yet, why are you calling to inform me of who is in my own home when you don't live here, neither do you have any say-so on who enters in and out of my house?* Red flag!

That type of behavior is indicative of a jealous personality, which is a real headache to deal with. For someone to watch everything you do and feel like they have the right to question and confront you about things that don't involve them, and about your personal life, especially when considering the fact that you're your own person, that's a sign that you're walking into a danger zone. Also, as time progressed, the questioning kept occurring. Questions would soon turn into accusations, and then accusations would later turn into something much worse.

Another red flag came one Saturday evening when Mike and I attended a party with family and friends—I left my kids at my mom's house. I was excited about having a good time. I went to grab something to drink; but when I returned, I noticed Mike and my brother were about to fight. I jumped in between the two to stop them from coming to blows. I later learned that Mike wanted to fight my brother because he discovered that my brother was sleeping with one of his baby mommas—yes, Mike already had children by several other women. After the altercation, Mike was upset the rest of the night although he decided to remain at the party. At one point, I noticed that one of my shoes came loose. When I bent over to tie my shoe, that's when the real

Finally Free

trouble began. At the time, I was wearing a two-piece short set with stringed up heels. When I'd bend over the top of my thong showed; this ticked Mike off. Furious that the top of my panties was showing, he hollered, "Stand your ass up—showing your panties!" That caught me by surprise—the fact that he felt comfortable talking to me so rudely. It's not like I was trying to show my panties deliberately; but even if I was, that still didn't give him the right to address me in that manner. Red flag! However, rather than check his attitude, I simply responded,

"I'm trying to tie my shoe."

"Let's go," he demanded after I stood up.

"But we just got here," I complained.

"I need to make a quick run somewhere. Let's go!"

I didn't view Mike's disrespectful attitude as a red flag at first. I just thought he was having a bad day. I know now that, regardless of what type of day he was having, there should have been a line established with regards to communication, one not to be crossed. Allowing someone to speak to you rudely and with disrespect, that's crossing the line. Letting someone take out their frustrations on you is a big red sign; it indicates that they'll most likely abuse you physically. Remember: Abusers will test you to see what they can get away with; and if they can get away with verbally disrespecting you, they'll feel comfortable physically assaulting you. They're trying to see what they can get away with.

When you spot this red flag, run for the hills. Things won't get better. Thinking that by giving in to their demand or demands, they will calm down and treat you with respect is a mistake. Not only will they continue to treat you unkind, but they'll feel more empowered to treat you disrespectfully.

Chapter 2: The Things We Choose To Ignore

The more you cave in to them, the meaner they'll become. A mousy attitude enables them to be more of a bully. When you demand that they respect you, letting them know early on that you won't settle for disrespect by any means, this will cause them to check their impulses at the door. Also, if they realize you mean business—meaning you'll end the relationship, involve the authorities, kick them out, and if need be, send them to meet their maker—then they will cut out their games and shape up or move on, but you can't play with them. You should never ignore them, as I did, saying things to yourself like "Oh, he's just angry," "He's never hit me before, so I'm not worried," and using other excuses to justify their bad behavior. Do not let "love" blind you to the truth about a person. That's why it's crucial that you wait before getting intimate with a person, giving your heart and body to them. You don't know what type of person they may be. You haven't seen them when they're angry, frustrated, or stressed out. You don't know how they'll cope with different situations. You need to examine them in different settings and observe how they interact with other people, especially their siblings and parents. The Bible tells us we can judge a tree by the fruit it bears, so pay attention to their fruit.

When you become sexually involved with a person, especially as a woman, your body releases certain chemicals that strengthen the bond between you and that person. That bond can impair your judgment and blind you to the character flaws of the individual. When you stay celibate, you'll find your judgment is not so darkened, and it will be much easier to separate from a toxic situation.

Concerning this particular red flag, another thing I need to point out is the fact that Mike felt comfortable with criticizing my clothes. It's like he had a responsibility to tell me how to dress. He used criticism as his tool of manipulation. Criticism is damaging to a person's self-image. It's used as a weapon by abusers to inflict shame on a person to break their spirit and make them despise their uniqueness.

Be cautious when dealing with an overly critical person. They'll try to beat you down with their words and make you feel ashamed of who you are. These type of individuals will always find something to complain about concerning you. If you change something about yourself just to satisfy them, they'll find something else you need to change about yourself. Realize that you're not the problem; they are. They are unhappy, and can't feel a sense of importance unless they're micromanaging and controlling everything you do.

Control-freaks suffer from a disease. They constantly crave power; and the more they get, the more they want. It's like a drug they can't break free from. Eventually, this *drug* will become their own demise if they don't get a handle on it, but that's their business. Your mission is to avoid feeling a sense of shame due to their antics. No one has the right to control your life, to determine what you wear, where you go, what you enjoy, what you watch, what you drive, where you live, and even who you choose to see. As long as your actions aren't violating another person's space and family, then you have the freedom to do *you*. Don't let anyone take that right away from you.

I noticed even more red flags as time progressed. For example, while at another get-together, I noticed a girl there who seemed to be drawn to Mike a little too much. I sensed there was something strange about how she was hanging all up under him, but I dismissed it from my mind, a decision

Chapter 2: The Things We Choose To Ignore

I'd later come to regret.

One of the biggest red flags Mike immediately displayed was his tendency to accuse me of unfaithfulness. That was an indication that he was insecure. Whenever we'd go out in public, he was always nervous that another man was looking at me or I was looking at someone else, then he'd confront out of fear and suspicion. He would say things like "Oh, so you looking at that dude?" "Why you smiling all up in that guy's face?" "So you sleeping with him or something?" At first, he'd act like he was playing, but he was serious. He was always questioning me about other guys. I found myself constantly having to explain myself—*'No, Mike. I'm not messing with him.' 'No, Mike, he's just someone I knew from back in the day.'* The problem was in his own mind, not my actions. Insecurity is a person's personal issue they must conquer on their own; their paranoia is their own problem. You are not responsible for curbing their fears and controlling what's in their head. Furthermore, if you remain in that situation and continue to allow them to get away with this bad behavior, it will grow progressively worse over time, as I found out.

I saw signs left and right, but I kept dismissing them. I began making excuses for Mike's behavior. I doubted my judgment, doubted my intuition, and I dismissed my observations, downplaying them in my mind. Never downplay what you see.

Oh, and regarding lines that should never be crossed… What happened next took things to a new level.

Finally Free

Points To Remember

- Don't get committed too soon when in a relationship. Don't have sex unless you're married. Furthermore, take it slow. Time will reveal what's on the inside of an individual.
- Watch how your partner behaves in different settings: in public, around their family, how they treat their parents, how they treat others. Take note of how they handle stress and conflict. If they can't handle conflict and stress, chances are they might not be able to handle you.
- Look for "Red Signs". If your partner tries to control you, verbally insults you, criticizes you constantly, questions your whereabouts and wants to keep track of everything you do, is always accusing you of being unfaithful, doesn't want you having friends, wants to isolate you from friends and family, wants to control who you talk to, and loves to guilt-trip you into doing what they want you to do, these are dangerous signs.

CHAPTER 3

THE FIRST HIT

THAT SATURDAY NIGHT AT THE PARTY, EVERYTHING went downhill. I was looking forward to having a good time, but Mike got angry and wanted to leave. Whether or not he was thinking about my brother or ticked off over the fact that part of my thong was showing through my outfit, I didn't know; but one thing I did know was I'd just witnessed a different side of the respectful, gentle, kind guy I hooked up with. We had been together for only three months, and he was already showing his jealous, possessive, insecure side. I never experienced this before. Although my ex-husband was a drug dealer, he was never insecure. He never spoke to me disrespectfully and acted jealous and possessive; therefore, Mike's actions took me by surprise. Even still, I didn't think too much of it.

We got in my Blazer and left the party that evening. Mike was driving. I didn't know where he was going, only

Finally Free

that he claimed he needed to make a "quick run" somewhere. While we were driving, I was staring out the window. Occasionally, I'd glance over at him, noticing anger written all over his face as he stared straight ahead. *What's going through his head?* I wondered to myself. He turned down a dead-end street. I didn't know what he was up to, where he was going. For all I knew, he was lost or wanted to find someplace private for the two of us to talk. I didn't know what was going on. *The house is that way. So why are we over here?*

While on that dead-end street, Mike parked the car. Darkness was all around us. You could only hear the sound of outdoors—crickets chirping, hooting owls, and other wildlife. In the car, there was a dead silence. Then suddenly, out of nowhere, "POW!!" It felt like fire shot through the side of my face, and my eyes saw a flash of light. At first, I didn't know what had happened; I was stunned, shocked; and then it dawned on me—*Mike just hit me!* However, before I could regain my composure, he punched me again, then again. He kept punching me with all of his might, aiming for my face. I lifted my arms to try and cover my face—my lip was busted. He landed blows on my arms, my shoulders, the side of my head, wherever he could. There was pure hatred in his eyes. "Please don't hit me!" I begged him, but he didn't say a word. He continued to punch me, his rage intensifying with every punch. He was like a man possessed; and yet, he was in full control of himself.

He had that planned. He wanted to get me alone, far away from the party attendees, away from my family, away from everyone so that he could unleash hell on me inside of own my vehicle.

Chapter 3: The First Hit

Losing My Fight

Now, I know what you're thinking: *'Why didn't you just fight back?'* Good question. That's the same question that's often asked to every woman and man who has been subjected to physical violence by a spouse, boyfriend, girlfriend, family member, or loved one. All of us wonder about that, including the victims.

Why didn't I fight back? That's the question I grappled with in my mind. Growing up, I wasn't the type of person to sit back and let someone bully me. I was a fighter. Like that line from *The Color Purple*, "All my life I had to fight!" That was me. I was the one who fought all through grade school. I was ready to throw down at all times. It didn't matter when. It didn't matter where. *So what happened, Ortavia?*

While Mike was beating me in that vehicle, all I could do was plead, scream, and cry. I couldn't even think. I felt somewhat numb, paralyzed by the shock I felt. I couldn't believe it. I couldn't believe that was happening. In a fight, you expect to get hit, but often, in cases of domestic abuse, the violence is sudden and unexpected and from an unexpected source. I didn't know what to do. I had never planned on being in this situation, so I didn't prepare for it. I was knocked off of my game, so I froze.

After beating me, Mike drove me home. I got out the vehicle, bloody and bruised, almost bewildered, dizzy, still somewhat in a state of disbelief. Mike then took off in my car, leaving me there alone. The look in his eyes was like that of a predator that had snagged its prey and buried it in a safe place with intentions on returning to finish it off. I knew it wasn't over; he wasn't done with me, yet. He felt like he had me where he wanted me; and sadly, he did. That night, after

Finally Free

I dragged myself through my front door, I thought about it: *This is the first time I have ever been in a fight where I didn't fight back.* That thought reverberated throughout my soul like the sound of a sonic boom, sending ripples through every fiber of my being. *I didn't even fight back,* I couldn't help but think.

I don't know which was worse: the beating Mike gave me or the one I gave myself? I did just as much, if not more, damage to myself than he did. I allowed shame and discouragement to overtake me, which was deadlier than any fist.

Emotional wounds run deeper than physical wounds. If someone punches you in the face, they might leave a mark on your face that's only skin-deep; however, when your soul is wounded, the damage is far more considerable and significant than any physical blow; and worse, it's hidden.

Many scientific journals reveal much about the damaging effects of emotional pain. Psychology Today printed an article entitled *5 Ways Emotional Pain Is Worse Than Physical Pain*, in which they explain how serious emotional pain is. In the article, they reveal that, unlike physical pain, emotional pain isn't physically visible, although it's equally as damaging. Physical bruises are visible, but not emotional ones; so people will often pay more attention to the physical bruises while ignoring and even minimizing the emotional scars; and yet, emotional bruises, according to the article, are the leading cause of low self-esteem and mental health issues. Also, emotional pain doesn't heal with time, whereas physical pain does. A busted lip will heal automatically. The swelling in a bruised eye will subside automatically. However, trauma doesn't heal automatically; and all it takes to trigger the emotional pain is a memory; this can put a person in the position where they relive the traumatic experience over

Chapter 3: The First Hit

and over again, which is torture. The same part of the brain that lights up when we experience physical pain is discovered to be the same part of the brain that lights up when we experience emotional pain.

I was traumatized and didn't know it. Psychological trauma, according to the American Psychiatric Association (APA), is *a type of damage to the mind that exceeds one's ability to cope and process the emotions they feel as a result of their experience.* It's like being stuck in a coma, unable to move. A traumatized person can't merely "snap out" of their distress; they must go through counseling to regain their confidence. Just look at soldiers returning home from war who're dealing with PTSD (Post Traumatic Stress Disorder). If you know someone who's undergone any type of abuse, whether it be physical, emotional, or psychological, treat them as one who's dealing with trauma and needs to undergo treatment at the hands of a trained counselor. Realize that it's not that they don't want to get over their pain; it's that they can't, at least, not without outside help.

That experience in the car left me mentally scarred. I couldn't deal with the shame I was experiencing. Furthermore, I didn't think I needed to sit down with someone (a professional or pastor) that could walk me through the steps to recovery. I thought I had all the power in myself to hoist myself out of my distress; and when I couldn't, I beat myself up for it. I didn't seek help after that incident. I just kept my mouth shut, and beat myself up for not *making* myself heal. I started to slip into a pit of toxic thoughts and eventually found it difficult to look myself in the mirror. I began to call myself a failure and a weakling. I even started to believe I deserved to be abused since I failed to stand up for myself. I

Finally Free

didn't realize that what Mike did to me wasn't my fault, and the trauma I experienced was beyond my control.

I felt disappointed in myself, and consequently, I lost respect for myself. I grew depressed. I felt like Rocky from the movie *Rocky III*: mentally defeated, discouraged, unable to rebound from a dissatisfying performance.

HUSH! DON'T TELL!

While at the apartment, I wrestled with whether or not I should reach out to someone for help, whether I should tell someone about what Mike did to me. I realized I needed to say something to someone, so I called a friend of mine. She didn't pick up her phone, so I left a lengthy message on her answering machine explaining everything that happened, but at the end, I begged her not to say anything to anyone about what I was sharing. After that, I laid down in the bed; tears were streaming down my face. I thought about calling my family. I knew they would have handled Mike, but I had my reservations about doing that. Not that keeping my family in the dark was the best decision I made, but there were certain concerns in my mind regarding involving my family in this situation, which I'll explain later.

Aside from my friend, there was one other person I felt comfortable with talking about the incident to, God. I can remember praying, "Lord, what have I gotten myself into?" Right then, Mike came home. It was late. Where was he? What was he doing all that time? I didn't know. I really didn't care. All I knew was I was scared to death of him. So I slept close to the edge of the bed with my back turned, afraid that he would grab me and hit me some more. Thankfully, he didn't attack me. I soon fell asleep—the last thought

Chapter 3: The First Hit

on my mind being *'Why didn't I fight back?'*

The next day, I got up and proceeded to move about as if nothing happened. I was in a state of denial about my situation, even telling myself that the abuse would only occur once and no more after that, but things were about to get worse. Mike had a strategy, a game-plan. You see, we had been in that apartment for only a few months—five months to be exact. The apartment was too close to home for Mike. I had too many family members close by, so he instructed me to look for another place for us to live. It had been over a month since he hit me. By not hitting me since that time in the car, I thought I was out of the danger zone, but I wasn't. He was taking me somewhere he'd be able to carry out his wrath without fear of getting caught. He tricked me with a false sense of security. I got another apartment, one that was more secluded; and now, I was isolated from my family and friends. Now, the real pain was about to begin.

Finally Free

Points To Remember

- Never feel guilty because someone else abused you. It's not your fault; therefore, don't allow guilt and shame to consume you due to someone else's actions. We're only responsible for what we do, not what other people do.
- Set standards early on in the relationship by communicating what you won't tolerate (i.e., physical abuse, insults, belittling, etc.).
- If someone hits you, don't expect things to get any better. It will get worst. Physical abuse is not a sign of love; it is a sign of disrespect.
- Be forgiving towards your abuser and yourself, but exercise wisdom and get out of that environment as quickly as possible. Involve the authorities if need be.

CHAPTER 4
MY TIME IN PRISON

My family might have been broke, but we were close. If you messed with one of us, you had to deal with all of us. Like I mentioned earlier, I was a fighter; that was well known throughout my family growing up. My siblings knew that I was not the type of girl to lie down and take crap from anyone; but in case anyone decided to bring it, they had my back.

One questions I get asked a lot whenever I share my story is "Why didn't you tell your family?" To most people, that would have been the simplest thing to do. *Sure, I didn't fight back, but I have family members that will gladly fight on my behalf. Why not involve them?* Makes sense, right? Well, for me, it wasn't that simple. I was afraid of Mike, but I was also afraid of a few other things too. I was living in fear. I allowed fear to sabotage me at every turn. Let me explain—

Finally Free

A PRISON OF FEAR

I had a reputation at home. Mom, dad, my brothers and sisters all knew me as the fighter in the family. They were confident that wherever I went, whomever I got involved with, whatever situation I found myself facing, I'd always stand up for myself. They didn't expect me to be in the situation I was in. I know this might sound a little strange, but I was more afraid of ruining my reputation than I was getting beaten. I didn't want my family to think less of me and see me as a helpless victim. To me, that would have been disappointing for them. I was fearful of defying their expectations.

To tell you the truth, I didn't know how my family would have responded to the news about my situation. Well, I knew to a degree what to expect from them, but not what they'd think about me. I just had a bunch of crazy thoughts running through my mind. It was as if the devil was feeding me ideas to keep me isolated in a prison of fear—*'If you tell your family about this, they'll judge you for it and look at you as a failure, as a disappointment.' 'If you try to leave, you'll never get away.' 'You deserve what you got because you're not worthy of more.'* I was in a prison of fear, afraid of getting hit by Mike, being judged by my family and losing my reputation, being a disappointment, being perceived as a failure, leaving the relationship, staying in the relationship; and furthermore, I was afraid of something terrible happening to Mike.

I did mention already that my family was close-knit, right? *Yeah, I did.* We looked out for one another, and I was aware of the fact that had I told them what Mike did to me, they wouldn't have taken it sitting down. I know for certain my family would have grabbed their pitchforks and torches, their axes, knives, guns, strapped rounds to their chests like

Chapter 4: My Time In Prison

Rambo and went on the rampage looking for Mike. It would have been the clarion call, "Off with his head!" I didn't want any harm to come to Mike. I was more concerned about his safety even though my safety was in jeopardy. I was trying to protect him even though I was the one that needed protecting.

Not only was I afraid of Mike getting hurt, but I was even afraid of hurting Mike's feelings—and his mom's. Satan fed me more thoughts to chew on, and I chewed them like a cow. I began telling myself that it would be devastating to Mike if I left him, especially considering he had just lost his brother to senseless violence and needed emotional support to help him cope with that tragedy. *Mike needs me*, I thought. *I need to be there for him.* I believed I was being selfless when what I was actually doing was being foolish. I was coming up with more reasons to stay in a toxic relationship. I minimized my feelings and exalted another's over mine as if my wants and needs didn't matter and my safety was less important than another person's convenience. That's the attitude of a person that doesn't value and respect him or herself. I know that we, women, are relational beings by nature, but the most important relationship you can have—besides one with God—is a relationship with yourself. If you don't love and value yourself, you'll never be virtuous enough to be there for your man in the way he truly needs you. If you don't respect yourself, a man won't respect you. I discovered that men learn to respect you when they see you respecting yourself—you teach them to treat you a certain way based on how you treat yourself. If you have standards, they will recognize their boundaries and adhere to those standards. If you have no standards, they will walk all over you as if you're

Finally Free

a sidewalk.

I failed to establish boundaries with Mike throughout our relationship. From the start, I gave him the impression that he didn't have to earn my trust. He didn't have to wait for sex and intimacy. I just let him move right into my apartment. I was too busy running from past hurts I didn't realize the future pain I was causing myself. Anger, not wisdom, was dictating my actions and decisions. When I should have spent time discovering who I was, who God designed me to be, and my value, I was being led by desperation and my fleshly impulses into one relationship after another; and each relationship was distracting me from the internal pain I needed to heal from.

Not only was I hesitant to leave because of the sudden murder of Mike's brother, but I convinced myself I would be doing his mother a disservice by leaving since the two of us had grown close by this time. I didn't want to leave her baby boy because it would hurt her heart and disappoint her. We talked a lot. She would share with me intimate things about her family, which made me feel close to them. We developed a mother-daughter bond that made it hard for me to leave; and yet, I was doing everything for everyone else, trying not let them down. The only person that I didn't have a problem with letting down was...me.

THE REAL ISSUE

My pride was really my downfall. That was the root of my problem, not fear. Fear may have played a major role in the decisions I made, but it was my pride that I was mostly concerned about. I wanted to maintain a certain image. I didn't want to look bad. I didn't want to look bad to Mike, to my

Chapter 4: My Time In Prison

family, and Mike's mom. I was more concerned about how I looked to others than I was how I looked to God and my own children. I could care less about God's best; I preferred people's best, their admiration, love, and respect.

Pride says, "It's all about me." Humility, on the other hand, is not what people think it is. It's not low self-esteem, self-abasement, and self-deprivation. Humility, as defined by the Bible, is *to make oneself low before God, to deny one's will while accepting His will*. In essence, humility is making God the center of our lives, not people. We are to let our lives revolve around God, and not God around our agendas and plans. That's the reality I had to face: it was all about me. I wanted other people's praises and love, even at the expense of not loving myself and embracing the woman I was created to be.

The Bible says, "For God has not given us a spirit of fear, but of love, and of power, and of a sound mind" (1 Timothy 1:7). Also, 1 John 4:18 says, "There is no fear in love; but perfect love casteth out fear: because fear hath torment. He that feareth is not made perfect in love." So, if being aligned with God's will for my life meant living a life of love, power, and soundness, then that also meant being out of alignment with God's will for my life led to fear, which brings torment. Being afraid of everyone, living in so much fear, was more of a spiritual issue than anything else, and I had to realize this and view it as such. I was living in a state of torment because my focus was on everything but the right thing.

Is it any coincidence that the letter "I" sits in the center of the word "pride"? No, it's not. That's also why pride is the one thing that drives us away from God. If I was going to survive, *I* was going to have to move out of the way and realize that abuse was, and will never be, a part of God's will for me. I also had to realize that living for the praise of others wasn't God's will for me. Even though it may hurt us, we must accept the fact that living in God's will may mean removing some people from our lives. It may hurt their feelings, but their being there will hurt your destiny. So you have to make a decision who you're going to hurt. Everyone isn't meant to be a part of your journey. Some people can't handle where God wants to take you. You can't please everyone; you shouldn't even try. Don't be concerned with having everyone like you. It's not about you. What does God think about you? What does He want to do with your life? That's the real question.

Another way pride controls us is through unforgiveness. Believe it or not, I was too unforgiving towards myself. I carried my shame around like it was a Loui Vuitton bag, guarding it with my life because it gave me an excuse to feel sorry for myself. We love to feel pitiful. We'll find the most ridiculous excuses to stay in the worst situations so that we can enjoy the fabulous joys of self-pity. *'If only my momma would have raised me better...' 'If only I had of...' 'If I would never have...' 'You don't know. You don't understand. You've never been there.' 'Nobody knows the troubles I've seen (bells).'* The truth is, we don't want to let go of our pain because it garners sympathy and support from others, it makes us feel like victims, and it justifies our not doing our part in life. We get to place blame on others when things aren't working out for us.

Pride made me believe it was my job to control everyone and everything. *It is up to me to control other people's actions*, I believed. *Therefore, Mike hitting me was my fault.* But that wasn't true. I couldn't control his actions. I could only

Chapter 4: My Time In Prison

decide what I was going to *continue* to put up with.

Since I didn't put an end to the abuse early, it became difficult for me to forgive myself; and yet, I'd somehow convinced myself that I was supposed to be a superwoman. I denied myself the privilege of making mistakes and assumed I'd never have to "get up" because I'd never "get knocked down." *Hey, I'm the fighter; I can't lose, nor would I ever end up being taken advantage of*, or so I thought. Now that I needed mercy, I didn't have any to give myself because I never thought I'd need any to cover my own blunders. So I didn't stand up to Mike when I should have, but that's okay. We all have regrets, but only those who know how to forgive and even capitalize on their mistakes, growing from them rather than crying over them, are the ones who come out on top in life. The best fighters are the ones that learn how to get back up after being knocked down. They don't sit on the canvas and cry because their opponents knocked them down. They jump up, shake the knockdown off, go back to their corner, and then come back for the next round with a new strategy.

What I should have been saying to myself is, "Okay. I let him get away with that, but that's fine because it won't happen again. He got me that time; I froze up, but he won't get away with that again. I forgive myself. I know now what I'm dealing with. No more!" Instead, I was telling myself, "I can't believe you let him do that to you." That was the problem. I kept putting myself down rather than building myself up. That's called negative self-talk, and it's dangerous.

Forgive yourself and choose to grow and learn from your mistakes rather than allowing your mistakes convince you that you are a mistake. No, you're not. Truthfully, you'll have a lot more failures; but if you commit to growing from

Finally Free

them rather than allowing them to define you, you'll regain the confidence and self-respect you lost. We all get hit in life, whether it be by circumstances or physical violence; but what determines whether or not you're a real fighter, a true champion, is whether you decide to learn from your mistakes and get up or stay down and mope over them. Fighters expect to get knocked down, but plan to get up. Realize that God created you to be a fighter, SO GET UP AND FIGHT!

It would be a long road ahead before I fully grasped what I'm currently telling you; actually, things began to get a whole lot worse before they got better. I'd have to hit rock bottom before realizing no one was going to *give* me my peace, joy, and freedom back, and that no one was going to *let* me live. I'd have to reach to brink of death before discovering that it was left to me to *take* these things back on my own.

Chapter 4: My Time In Prison

Points To Remember

- Fear is like a prison cell; it will restrict your movements in life. Realize that fear is only in the mind. Once you break free from fear, you'll realize that there's no one and nothing available that can hold you back. Choose not to live in fear.
- Repeat this after me: "God has not given me a spirit of fear, but of love, power, and of a sound mind. I denounce the spirit of fear and choose to walk in the love, power, and soundness of God today!"
- Drop your pride and focus on serving God rather than impressing people. You can't please everyone, nor were you designed to. Focus on pleasing God and don't waste anymore of your time on people who don't mean you any good.
- Forgive yourself for your mistakes and forgive others for their mistakes and choose to move on and live your life. Focus on God's future for you rather than your past mistakes.
- SPEAK UP! Break the silence and tell someone if you are experiencing physical abuse in your relationship.

Finally Free

CHAPTER 5

A NEW LOW

I WAS PLUMMETING INTO A PIT OF EXCUSES; THEY WERE the only things that could help me stay with Mike at this point. *'His brother died. We needed each other.'* Also, there were more to come as time progressed, such as *'he was raised in an abusive household, witnessing his father beat his mom. So that's why he does what he does.'* More revelations about Mike kept coming down the pipeline. I felt like I was obligated to stay now out of sympathy, out of pity. *'Poor Mike.'*

By this time, the beatings had become routine. Getting punched, slapped and kicked, thrown against the wall and insulted to my face, this became my reality; and yet, my biggest concern was making sure my family didn't know about what was going on, and making sure the abuse didn't take place in front of my girls. Mike was conscious of their presences too. He'd make sure to beat me in the room with the door closed or when the girls were away. Still, how many

Finally Free

lies can you tell your kids? How many excuses can you come up with to explain a busted lip and other bruises? The door hit you? You tripped and fell on your face? A bee stung you on the lip? You tripped over a banana peel and busted your head? Think about it. Furthermore, how naive do you think children are? Do you think they believe the lies you tell them when you happen to show up with fresh bruises on your face and arms? *Really?*

Mike was scared of getting caught. He'd hit me in the face sometimes, but not often. Mostly, he'd hit me below the neck—that's where the bruises would be. He didn't want the evidence of his barbarism to be visible. However, at home, it was evident what was going on. The thuds against the wall and door followed by crashing sounds and other noises indicating that physical violence was taking place could easily be heard coming outside of our door.

I was afraid that my girls would one day hurt Mike, even kill him for what he was doing to me. That concerned me. I didn't want to expose them to what was going on, but at the same time, I couldn't shield them from reality—it was happening in our own home. I went from being beat *because* to being beat *just because*. He didn't need an excuse anymore. I was busy creating new excuses to justify his behavior while he was gradually dismissing all of his excuses.

I began expecting beatings although I dreaded them. Mike would be kind for a little while after beating me, and then he'd unleash hell again. This became as common to me as the simple tasks of eating, drinking, breathing, and sleeping. I was now in clean-up mode. I spent time doing nothing but hiding, lying, making excuses, and faking. I wasn't even attempting to prevent the abuse from happening anymore.

Chapter 5: A New Low

I wasn't even expecting to live a life free of abuse. I began to do the worst thing imaginable: accept it. That was an indication that I had given up on my bright destiny. It was like I was floating off of fumes; staring in the mirror at the hollow shell of a woman that once had a promising life and future, a woman who was once full of ambition as a girl. That woman was dead now. The only woman staring back at me from the other side of the mirror was a soul-less drone who had finally been reduced to nothing but a living, breathing punching bag for another man to unleash his anger on. But I did have my girls. They were my reason to continue living, but what would I pass on to them? What could they learn from their mother at this point? They didn't see strength, vitality, vivaciousness. They didn't see a woman roaring like a lioness; but rather, a kitty cat purring and balling up in the corner in the presence of a large, menacing shadow. I felt powerless in my own life and was now feeling useless as a mother; and worse, the wave of revelations about Mike kept crashing into the side of my existence like the waves of a sea against an old ship, knocking it from side to side.

I knew about Mike's other children from his previous relationships, but I didn't think he was still messing with any of his old baby mommas or any other women. Do you recall the girl I told you about in chapter two who kept hanging all up under Mike while we were at a get-together? Well, as it turned out, my suspicions were right. A woman's intuition is to be trusted. That girl wasn't all up under him for nothing. He was cheating on me with her.

Mike was chasing tail in the streets while giving me hell at home. He continued to stay out all night at the clubs. He would accuse me of sleeping around if a guy even looked

Finally Free

my way. He even beat me once because someone called the house and hung up after realizing they had the wrong number. When the person hung up, Mike accused me of being on the phone with another guy and discreetly playing it off as if it was a wrong number. After beating me, he dialed the number back only to discover it indeed was a wrong number—and he never apologized for it. He was always accusing me of cheating, but you know what they say: *If a person is continuously accusing you of something, chances are they're the ones guilty of it.* Mike would pick out my panties. He wanted me to wear what he called "church panties"—he figured they'd be less flattering and less tempting to other men. If I stayed in church longer than the expected time, Mike would accuse me of sleeping with the pastor. I was repeatedly being accused of cheating and monitored for underwear violations even as panties were constantly showing up in our mailbox.

Mike was still sexually active with several of his baby mommas; that's who he was ordering all of those panties for since they weren't for me. When Mike was asleep or away, his baby mommas (who he would be with at the time) would pick up his cell phone and call my house just to play and rub it in my face that he was with them. The facade was getting too heavy. In front of our families and friends, I was a happy woman who was always on point with the kids and the house, always making sure it was tidy and clean, making sure dinner was prepared and the household business was taken care of. The outside world looked at me marveled. Everyone thought I was living a beautiful life, but I was living a lie and experiencing pure hell; but I made sure no one knew it. That was my main job, and I did my *job* well. The weight, however, was starting to bear down on me, and I was reach-

Chapter 5: A New Low

ing my breaking point.

My world was shrinking. The walls were closing in on me. It was all about Mike—what he wanted, his temper, his way. It was like I was the vanishing woman. Other men were afraid to come near me. I couldn't breathe no matter where I went. Even at school, I remember standing next to one of my classmates while on a short break when I suddenly got a text message from Mike asking me who was the boy standing next to me in the hallway. Mike was stalking me as if he didn't have a job; or better yet, as if controlling me was his job. If I went to the club, he'd have people spy on me to see if anything happened (i.e., another guy hitting on me). If a guy got too close to me, he'd accuse me of flirting. One night at the club, he jumped up in a fit of rage and tried to fight a guy he claimed touched my butt. It was dumb because it was my brother's childhood friend he accused of feeling on me. Another night, my family came over and took me out to the club, but Mike being Mike, he showed up about thirty minutes later and told me to get in the car. My family wanted me to stay, but I came up with a lame excuse to leave with Mike much to their displeasure. While in the car, he tried to play reverse psychology on me by saying, "You're a church girl. You don't belong in the club."

Mike's control over my life was suffocating, but what was suffocating me the most was the silence—I wouldn't tell a soul about what I was going through. That's what drove me to the edge. That's the destructive power of silence: it destroys you from within. The longer I stayed quiet, the harder it got to break the silence and say something to someone. By this point, I felt like I'd dug a pit for myself that was too steep to climb out of, so I began entertaining the thought of

Finally Free

checking out of life altogether.

THE ULTIMATE HUMILIATION

Amazingly, after everything Mike put me through, I still hoped there was a shred of love and respect in our relationship. I tried to salvage what pieces of love and intimacy that existed in our relationship that could still be found. I wanted to work things out the best I could. I wanted some semblance of normalcy at this point. I still wanted to feel like a lady; to be respected, caressed, romanced, and made to feel special. So I planned a candlelight dinner for the two of us and sent the kids away with his mother. If there was a spark that could be rekindled between us, I was determined to ignite it. Maybe this would create a fire in our relationship that would bring about a change. I put on my heels, my sexy dress, my makeup, and my lipstick so that I could feel like a queen for a night. I had everything set for us. Mike showed up for our date, but he wasn't alone. He brought his friend over to show him what I'd planned for the two of us. To me, that was a slap in the face. This night was supposed to be our night; it was supposed to be just us. My patience was being put to the test, but it was Mike's next transgression that led me to a new low.

Later, the two of us were at home relaxing when the phone rang. Mike answered. His homeboy was on the other line. Mike had his ways, he had his problems, but whenever some of his friends came around, they seemed to turn the dial up even more. They would influence him to act out in ways that shocked me even after all this time. It was apparent that he valued their opinions and lived for their praises and approval. They knew how to egg him on. When he an-

Chapter 5: A New Low

swered the phone, his friend wanted him to go and hangout. Mike expressed to him that he was trying to chill at the house with me. That's when his friend uttered those magic words: "Man, you must be pussy-whipped?" At that point, Mike's demeanor changed. He stuck out his chest and determined in his mind he was going to prove his friend wrong. Once he hung up the phone, he got dressed without saying anything to me about where he was going and then shot out of the apartment. He was gone. Where was he off to? Don't know. He stayed out for quite some time. What was he doing? Don't know that either. All I know is he ended up coming home late that night and woke me up out of my sleep. He seemed upset, or agitated. After abruptly waking me up out of my sleep, he asked me to perform oral sex on him, which is something I'd never done. I thought he was joking, so I ignored him and laid back down. Then he uttered,

"What man can't come home and get head from his lady?" I didn't know what was going on in his mind, whether he was drunk or high; but I certainly wasn't about to do what he was asking me to do. I continued to lie there, hoping he'd go and cool down, but he didn't; instead, he became aggressive and forcefully grabbed me and hollered, "You're going to give me some head!" He then pulled out a gun and placed it to my head. Then he forced me off the couch and onto my knees, unzipped his pants, pulled out his penis, and forced me to open my mouth; he then shoved his penis into my mouth, causing me to gag while choking me. He had no concern for how I felt. Then the thought came to my mind, *I wonder where his penis has been tonight?* The look in his eyes was almost otherworldly, like a man drunk with power and filled with rage. He wanted nothing more than to prove to me in that moment that I meant absolutely nothing to him; and that in his eyes, I was lower than the lowest species of animal walking the face of the earth, undeserving of respect. He wanted to demonstrate to me that I was nothing but an object for him to use in whatever way he saw fit. That was the most humiliating experience of my life.

With the gun still to my head, he took his other hand and pushed my head down to the floor and started to stomp on it. He stomped all over my body as if he hated me. I felt disgusting. Tears flowed from the corners of my eyes and watered the carpet. My heart bled. I'd never felt this low before. There I was again, numb internally. My voice, locked in a cage of silence, just waiting to burst out into a scream, began to quiet within me. My thoughts were in a state of suspended animation, no longer swirling around in my head. There was nothing else to think or consider, no beauty to behold. I felt dead inside. While he stomped all over me, it was as if there was nothing else for him to stomp out of me.

THE INVESTIGATION

A new revelation about Mike's infidelity came, this time it involved someone from my own family. I was told Mike was having an affair with my sister. That was gut-wrenching. My heart dropped into my stomach. I'd finally found something worse than death. *Another women?* No. *It's my own flesh and blood family, my sister? My sister!* The dagger already protruding out of my back was just thrust deeper and further than ever before. Even against my better judgment, I tried to tell myself this one couldn't be true. *It can't be!* I had to find out.

I didn't confront Mike about this one, not a first. Instead, I set out to do my own investigation, knowing he'd

Chapter 5: A New Low

just deny everything. So I began to ask around. One of my daughters shared with me a key piece of the puzzle; she said that she witnessed Mike entering into my sister's house one night, but then she stated that many people would go to her house; it was a hang out spot for Mike and his friends.

I continued to ask around. Finally, I jumped up and decided to go over to my sister's place to confront her about the matter. When I arrived, she was standing outside talking to my brother's baby momma. I got out of the car and asked her if she was having an affair with my man. She denied it, but then got angry and made a big deal out of my approaching her with the accusation. There was a load of tension in the air between us. Even before asking her about the situation, I could sense the tension; it was as if they were already talking about me behind my back before I even arrived. So, quite naturally, my being there and asking her if something was going on only escalated the tension. My brother's baby momma and I ended up getting into a shouting match, which then drew the attention of others, including a friend of my ex-husband's. My sister claimed that I went there to fight her over Mike, even though that wasn't the case. I just wanted answers.

After confronting my sister, I finally went home to confront Mike. At the time, his uncle was over at the apartment. Mike was on the couch while his uncle and I were in the kitchen. Of course, Mike denied everything, and just like my sister, he acted offended that I'd even bring up something of the kind and ask him about it. Our voices escalated, and then he picked up a glass and threw it at my head. I ducked just in time; it shattered all over the cabinet. I left the scene and went to the bedroom. After a while, I took a shower. Once finished, I hopped on the phone and called my uncle who was like a dad and shared with him the situation concerning Mike, my sister, and my suspicions. He just downplayed the situation, claiming that people were jealous of me and Mike's *beautiful* relationship and wanted to see it torn up. *Boy, was he wrong!* He did acknowledge that if that indeed were the case (Mike sleeping with my sister), then that would be extremely low and that I didn't deserve that, and encouraged me to continue to live my life. Little did he know my dignity and sanity were hanging on by a thread at that point due to all that Mike had put me through.

After Mike and his uncle left, a visitor that was close to us stopped by. They revealed to me the truth about what was taking place. They explained to me that Mike and my sister were sleeping together. Upon receiving this information, my whole world came crashing down. I was filled with anxiety, panic, anger, and more negative emotions. It was almost hard to breathe. *What am I going to do? What's going on? What's going on with my life?* Then, I had a sudden thought—

THE FINAL EXIT

My heart was rushing. My mind was foggy. Staggering dizzily, I rushed into the bedroom to grab a bottle of pills. Every ounce of me cried out for me to stop, but I couldn't. How else could I make the pain end? My chest felt like it caved in while a knot filled my stomach like a heavy stone. With adrenaline coursing through my veins and a demonic chant ringing through my ears, I opened the bottle. *Don't think about it! Just do it!* And so, I did. I tossed a handful of pills into my mouth and swallowed them in a frenzy, like a ravenous shark devouring chum in blood-infested waters. Silence

Chapter 5: A New Low

filled the air like a heavy mist. What forms and shapes I could make out through the blurred vision of my teary eyes began to be swallowed up by an encroaching blackness that gradually swept through the room like a thick, black shadow.

Everything then faded to black. Total silence. Total darkness.

Finally Free

Points To Remember

- Stop making excuses for someone else's bad behavior. Let them take responsibility for their own actions.
- They were living before they met you and they'll go on living without you. Don't think people can't make it without you. Everyone's happiness is not your responsibility.
- Realize that your children will be mentally and emotionally scarred as a result of watching you get abused, even if you think you're hiding it from them. Don't keep them in that kind of environment.
- Suicide is never the way out of a bad situation; turning to and trusting God is the way out. Think about those who're depending on you before you selfishly end your life. Furthermore, realize that there are brighter days ahead of you.

CHAPTER 6
EVERYBODY PLAYS THE FOOL

"LIVE, ORTAVIA!"

What's going on? Who—

"Ortavia, you will live and not die."

Who's—

"You will LIVE and NOT DIE!"

Wha—What? Where...where am I?

I snapped out of *it*. Now conscious but hazy, I was observing my surroundings, but I was barely able to make out anything. It's like I'd awakened from a dream, from a deep sleep that had fallen over me, draining me of every ounce of strength. I could barely feel my body. My arms felt like logs, too heavy to move. My legs felt like they were being held down with cinder blocks. *What just happened?* I wondered.

As my clarity of mind returned, I began to recall

Finally Free

much of what happened although some parts were still a blur. I was in my bedroom. *How did I get here? How did I end up on the bed?* I couldn't remember. Up until that point, some memories were vague, but I did remember rushing into the bedroom to get some pills, and then...

That's when it hit me, what I had done. I attempted the unthinkable. I just tried to kill myself. I noticed that an empty bottle of pills was in my hand. I was shocked but also upset. It was both a bitter-sweet feeling that death had passed over me. It slowly came back to me not only what I just did, but why I did it. Just the mentioning of *his* name in my mind was like a smelling sauce ushering in a rude awakening. *He's* what I just tried to escape. Still, the bitterness didn't begin to set in until I realized what else I nearly left behind. Immediately, the thought of my three girls rushed into my mind. *Oh, my God! Please don't tell me I was about to lose them! Or they were about to lose me! No!* I had never felt more terrible than at that moment. This feeling was worse than the throbbing pain of any heartbreak a man could bring, worse than any heart-wrenching disappointment a sister could bring. Those girls were my flesh and blood; they were my life. It's interesting how you don't realize how much a person means to you until you come close to losing them. I had forgotten all about them. For the last couple of months, they'd been more of an afterthought, playing the role of three supporting actresses in the ongoing drama that was me and Mike's relationship.

TYLER PERRY, MARY J. BLIGE, AND JESUS
The words in my head, while I was semiconscious, kept replaying in my mind—*"You shall live and not die."* Those words

Chapter 6: Everybody Plays The Fool

spoke to me from a place I hadn't known. It wasn't my voice. I wasn't trying to muster up the strength to hoist myself out of that dark pit of desperation. I didn't have the will to live, to press on. There was something or *someone* else that was determined to see me live, and to reach down into my body and breathe new life into it.

In church, I would hear about the person of the Holy Spirit, how He will talk to you at times, especially when you least expect Him to. His voice is described as being small, and still; it's characterized by gentleness and quietness that calls for the mind to quiet down to discern it. Well, my mind was quiet enough; my body still enough. I had nothing there to distract me where I was. He had all of the access to me that He needed at that moment. All I could do was lie there and listen to Him whisper into my ear those precious words.

His words revived me. The Holy Spirit saved me. All I could do was weep at the time, thinking about how precious and loved I am by God. *God truly loves and cares for me.*

When Mike came home, he discovered me laying nearly lifeless on the bed with a bottle of pills in my hand; that must have scared him to death. It didn't cross his mind to rush me to the hospital; instead, he hovered over me like a nervous wreck, trying to see if I was okay. I was alive, but the weight of death was still on me. Gradually, I began to regain my strength. I could feel my body again. Just then, the worst stomach ache I'd ever felt hit my belly and I ran to the toilet. It came up like lava from a volcano—a load of vomit. That happened a few more times throughout the night.

In the upcoming days, I found myself going through big time. My sister and I were no longer on speaking terms; even my mom stopped talking to me. My family would talk about me rather than talk to me. That was tough, but I had to remain strong; and yet, I still didn't want to live. I secretly prayed for God to take my life. I loved my daughters, but I wanted to die. *Perhaps, they'll end up in much better hands,* I hoped.

One day, I was thinking of ways to end my life without causing such a mess. Actually, there's no clean way to commit suicide. Regardless of how you pull it off, the lives of those connected to you will be uprooted by it, some even destroyed. That's the problem with the suicide-driven mind: it's only focused on what's directly in front of it rather than what's up the road. There are better days ahead, and there are other lives at stake. I was trapped in a delusion, contemplating another way out when it crossed my mind to watch Tyler Perry's *Madea's Family Reunion*. They say that laughter is medicine; I can't argue with that. That play was medicine to me. I laughed and reflected as several of the scenes struck home with me. I saw myself in many of those scenes, and the play reminded me that God is the real way out of the hell we find ourselves going through. I saw forgiveness acted out, and I saw freedom displayed. Even though it was acting, the message was clear: *Turn to God, forgive others, and walk in love.*

After that, I watched several of Tyler Perry's plays. *Madea* mixed with a little Mary J. Blige and a renewed passion for God's presence revived something on the inside of me. I felt new life entering into me. Hope was rising in me. Staying in church brought about the biggest change in my life. My perspective was changing. I began to realize that God wasn't trying to give me strength for a journey He never intended for me to take. God wasn't trying to get me to "be strong" while playing house with a man that didn't love

Chapter 6: Everybody Plays The Fool

and respect me; He was trying to get me to be wise and stop "playing house" altogether and instead focus on discovering His plan for me. I was trying to get Him to fix Mike, but He was trying to fix me so that I'd stop settling for something that wasn't supposed to be a part of my life to begin with. I needed to come out of sin also, rather than allowing my sin to rob me of God's best. That's the revelation I received.

Little by little, through the teaching of the Word of God on Sundays and during Bible study, God began to peel away the layers of lies that enshrouded me. I was being set free in my mind. I once was dead, but now I was alive. I was once blind, but now I was starting to see. It was all lies! Lies! Being told by Mike that he loved me was a lie! Him claiming that he had my back was also a lie! Him telling me that no one else would want me if I ever left him was a huge lie! All of Mike's lies were being exposed. I felt so refreshed and revived while listening to the truth, even though Satan still had a hold on me. The fight was far from over.

FOOLING MYSELF

God told me to leave—*Just leave! Take the girls and go!* The emphasis wasn't even on Mike; it was on me. I needed to come out of sin. There are some things you have to simply let go of before you can experience true freedom in your life. You can't be blessed while still holding on to cursed things (2 Corinthians 6:14). You have to let go of them. I was living with a man I wasn't married to. I needed to let that go. I was caught up into fornication. God told me to let that go. That's the definition of "repent"—it means "to turn away from". I needed to turn my back on sin, no matter who it was with—Mike or any other guy. Still, I allowed sin to remain in my

Finally Free

life, and the lure of sin sent me right back to the slave pit. I was on my way out of the door. I'd informed Mike that my girls and I were gone for good, but the enemy crept in and convinced me to disobey God's voice. It wasn't so much the begging that Mike did. It wasn't the empty promise to never hit me again. It wasn't his promise to change and be a better man. It wasn't even about Mike. It was my insistence on not obeying God, not trusting Him. I was stubborn. That's why I chose to stay in that hell-hole.

I can hear you now, asking, "Why in the world would you stay in a situation like that?" When a person is living in sin, they'll always open themselves up to the deceptions of the devil. There is no way to clean up sin. You can't give sin a makeover and expect its nature to change, neither can you expect God's best while living wickedly. No need to blame others; this is our responsibility to bear.

When God says move, you should move. Don't think about it and try to come up with reasons why you shouldn't do what He is instructing you to do. Don't try to rationalize things in your mind. Just obey. God knows what's best. We may think we have things figured out, we may think we can transform others and change situations on our own, we may think we can rely on our own strength and intellects rather than lean on God's, but that's a mistake. Obedience to God's instructions is what leads us into blessings and allows us to avoid curses and the traps set for us by the enemy.

Why did I stay? It's because I was blind. Sin blinds us. The Bible tells us in 2 Corinthians 4:4 that Satan "blinds the minds of them who believe not" the truth of God's Word. You can't get angry with a blind person for walking into a pit—they're blind! Moreover, you can't get angry with blind

Chapter 6: Everybody Plays The Fool

people who lead other blind people—they're all blind! Your mother might advise you to remain in a dangerous situation, your father may also give you this advice; don't be surprised. It's not like they see what God sees. They don't! When we're blind, we always allow our flesh to fool us into thinking we know what's best for ourselves and others; and as opposed to walking in wisdom, we rely on our wits and intellect, and that's what gets us into trouble.

I decided to listen to my thoughts rather than God's voice. I tried to be cunning, thinking that I could fix Mike. *Maybe my being here will prompt him to change his ways. Perhaps he'll realize he had a good thing. Maybe...* That was me trying to be smart. I was playing the fool while the devil laughed.

There we were, back together again. Mike acted differently...at the beginning, which is typical in many cases of abuse and domestic violence. An abuser will usually act good for a short while until they feel comfortable with going back to their old ways; and just as you probably suspected, it didn't take Mike long to return to his old ways. We would be at home together, enjoying one another, and then his old buddies would call. Even if he didn't want to leave, they had a way of manipulating him into doing what they wanted—usually by challenging his ego, making him think he was soft if he didn't go along with them. Then suddenly, it was back to the streets, the clubs, to drinking and doing drugs, to ignoring the kids and me. He'd hang out with them all night and then act a fool with me all day. One night, while hanging out with them, they were involved in a shootout. Mike got shot. He was afraid of his mom finding out he had been shot, undoubtedly because she'd already lost one son due to senseless violence. When I went to the hospital to pick him up, I was mad because he was so weak-minded and kept getting into trouble because he couldn't tell his friends no.

I was growing more and more frustrated with Mike's antics. He was back to his old ways and my kids were affected by it. For example, he would go out and get himself something to eat but wouldn't care that the kids were hungry and the refrigerator was empty. I would have to rush home from work to see about them because he wouldn't even see about them. On top of that, he got a new baby momma—and I was still getting calls from his old baby mommas all time of day and night. It was now time for Mike to go, so I asked him to leave, and surprisingly, he did without putting up a fight. That's probably what he wanted anyway since he had several women on the side he wanted to hook up with. He went and got his own place, and the two of us remained separated for a little while.

ANOTHER BIG BLOW

It wasn't long before Mike and I were under one roof again. We came back together to wait out a big hurricane that was about to hit our area. After the storm finally passed, we were left without power. Mike didn't act responsibly during this time, either. He was right back to his old ways: hanging out with his friends all night and neglecting the household. This time, things were a little different at home since he brought one of his daughters to live with us. I was now taking care of four girls while Mike ran the streets.

During this time, I was working in a doctor's office. I had a history of suffering from ovarian cysts, endometriosis, and fibroids, all of which caused unbearable pain whenever my menstrual cycle came on. Sometimes, the pain would be

Chapter 6: Everybody Plays The Fool

so intense it would have me balled up in the fetal position. One day, while my cycle was on, I experienced a pain I never felt before. My brother rushed over and took me to the hospital to get seen. He stayed right there by my side the whole time; but after the results of the examination were revealed, I wished he hadn't stayed. The results rocked me to my core. I found out I had contracted an STD. *From where? From who?* There was only one person that could have given it to me.

That was a new experience for me. I was well aware of STDs and their symptoms—I graduated Valedictorian from my nursing school—but never in a million years did I think I would be the one being told by a doctor, "You have an STD." This news floored both my brother and me. I was speechless; my brother was furious. He jumped up and stormed out of the room. Feeling ashamed, all I could do was drop my head and cry. I'd become accustomed to doing that a lot, crying. Whenever Mike cursed me out, I'd cry. Whenever beaten, I'd find myself just laying down and crying. And now...

After receiving the bad news about my health, I called Mike and asked him if he was cheating on me—as if I didn't already suspect that. I just wanted to see if he'd ever come honest and clean. Of course, as usual, he denied everything. He even pretended to be offended by the very fact that I'd think such a thing. Also, to make matters worse, when I got home, he displayed his anger towards me through his typical acts of violence for even questioning him about that issue.

By working in a doctor's office, I had access to treatment and medication to help with my condition. It dawned on me that Mike had been taking penicillin; he said he was doing it to clean out his system. He had this disease for some time. It hurt me that he slept with me while knowing that he had an STD. He demonstrated that he cared nothing about my health and safety; but, then again, he already proved that multiple times. How can someone abuse you, hit you, curse you, and cheat on you and still claim to love and care about you? That's not love; it's an indication that someone doesn't respect you. The Bible says a husband is supposed to love his wife as Christ loves the church (Ephesians 5:25). Christ sacrificed Himself for us. He doesn't abuse us. 1 Peter 3:7 says,

> "In the same way, you husbands must give honor to your wives. Treat your wife with understanding as you live together. She may be weaker than you are, but she is your equal partner in God's gift of new life. Treat her as you should so that your prayers will not be hindered." (NLT)

God commands wives to honor, respect, and obey their husbands, and husbands to give themselves sacrificially for the benefit and good of their wives, and furthermore, to respect and honor their wives the same way they would their own bodies. That's what Paul meant in Ephesians 5:28, which says,

> "In the same way, husbands ought to love their wives as they love their own bodies. For a man who loves his wife actually shows love for himself." (NLT)

So, if you're with a man who hates himself, how do you think he will treat you? He'll treat you with hatred and contempt. If he'll abuse himself with drugs, alcohol, promiscuous sex, and turn his back on God, then he'll abuse and mistreat you.

Chapter 6: Everybody Plays The Fool

If a man doesn't have a relationship with God, how can he know his true identity and purpose? He can't. Furthermore, if he doesn't know who he is—and is supposed to be—then how can you expect him to value you as a woman?

I know you're probably thinking, *Why would you hook up with a man who doesn't respect you? If you knew he didn't care about you and you suspected that he was already messing around on you behind your back, why did you put up with him?* You have to realize that I didn't understand who I was; I didn't respect myself either. When you, as a woman, don't respect yourself, you'll let others disrespect you; you'll let others walk all over you and then accept it as a norm, especially if you have low self-esteem and feel like no one else wants you. Low self-esteem is a byproduct of not knowing who you are. You don't know your worth; and hence, you feel worthless and deserving of disrespect. When you don't respect yourself, you don't have any standards; and when you lack standards, you'll let others step all over you without fear of consequences. You can't build your self-esteem up by getting into a new relationship. The only way you can build your self-esteem is by coming into the revelation of your true identity and worth, and this revelation can only be provided to us by our Creator, God.

Thankfully, God saw my pain and heard my silent cries. He was preparing to rescue me, and this rescue would start from within—with Him opening my eyes to the truth about myself and who I was always supposed to be. He was about to remove the scales from my eyes and save my life.

Finally Free

Points To Remember

- Stop believing the lies abusers tell you, such as "No one will want you besides me," "You're ugly and undesirable. You'll never have it better than me," "You won't make it on your own," I'm the only one that truly loves and cares about you," "I love you, but sometimes you make me do this to you because you won't do what I tell you. If you'd just do what I say, I wouldn't have to hit you," "I own you. You'll never get away from me," "You're worthless, useless," "You're stupid," and more.
- Tell yourself the opposite. In fact, speak this after me: "I am beautiful, smart, courageous, desirable; loved by others, especially God; resourceful, talented, and designed by God to succeed. I am not a failure, nor am I dependent on someone else for my provisions. God is my provider. He will never let me down. I will make it. I deserve God's best, not abuse and neglect. I am worthy of better. I refuse to settle for second-best."
- When you leave a bad relationship, don't look back. Keep going. Don't be fooled by empty promises, and don't just think about the good times. Remember the hell that person put you through.
- Spend time in church and with God's Word, discovering your true identity in Christ.

CHAPTER 7

THE DEVIL ALWAYS COMES BACK

I WAS LIVING LIKE A MARRIED WOMAN WITH A HOUSE full—four kids, three of them mine and one Mike's. I had two jobs. I was working at the doctor's office throughout the week and at a hair salon on the weekends. *Mike?* Well, he was being his typical self, which was wearing me out again. I didn't want to pretend anymore to be a family, living with a man that wasn't my husband, a man that didn't love me. I developed a longing for the real thing. It's like a light bulb came on inside of my head and my soul began to thirst for more than the cheap imitation life I had been clinging on to for so long.

I thought long and hard about my life. Perhaps, it was the last incident that caused me to reach my breaking point. Perhaps, it was the realization that Mike wasn't changing, at least, not anytime soon. Maybe it was just the epiphany that my life was at a total standstill that settled in my mind. I was hungry for more in life. I knew there was more to life than what I was experiencing. There had to be more. Much more. I didn't want to die unfulfilled, not anymore. While pondering this in my mind, I started to plan my escape. I thought about where I would go. Secretly, I began looking up shelters.

When you're in a toxic relationship that's not God's will for you, just know that there's no such thing as 'no way out.' You can get out of it no matter how long you've been in it. I slipped into a habit of playing house for a long time until one day I woke up and realized that's all I was doing, playing. After that, it dawned on me that the only person keeping me in that situation was myself. There were no physical prison bars and no jailers with shotguns standing guard 24/7. The only cage I was living in was fear, and that was only a state of mind; therefore, to break out of that cage, all I needed to do was have a change of mind. The words of the minister in the church and the words of Tyler Perry's plays began playing in my head again. God was bringing it all back to my mind. *There's more for you, Ortavia. I have so much more for your life, more that I want to give you, show you, and do in and through you. Don't settle for this.* I could hear God's voice in my spirit telling me this.

When deciding to escape these situations, you have to have an exit plan. Do your research and find out where to go. Look for shelters. Look for hotlines that have counselors that can walk you through developing a step-by-step plan of escape. Even as you engage in this activity, you'll find your courage building. After locating where to go, plan the timing for your exit. Will it be when he or she is asleep? Away at

Chapter 7: The Devil Always Comes Back

work? At the gym? Be methodical. Know that you *must* get out, for your life depends on it. Your children's lives may depend on it. Also, realize that sometimes unexpected things will happen, so don't be alarmed and don't lose your cool. Keep a level head, play it cool, be discreet, and ask God for His guidance and wisdom in executing a plan of escape.

While I was planning my escape, I grew more determined to follow through with it—this wouldn't be just another idea that fizzled out like a flash in the pan and became an afterthought. I talked to myself and encouraged myself, saying not only *could* I do it, but I *will* escape that situation. I WILL! I envisioned myself executing the plan successfully. This became my obsession. I'd confided in a friend of mine that I was going to a shelter. That may have been a mistake. *Who knows?* Sometimes, we share our plans with people only for them to betray our trust. Most times, it's wise to be quiet and *just do it*. In either case, I stayed the course and had everything set up. All I needed now was to wait for the perfect timing to follow through with everything.

Around this time, R&B artist R. Kelly was scheduled to be in town for a concert. He's known for one song in particular, *When A Woman's Fed Up*. That had become my mantra. I was an angry Black woman who was fed up. I was now desperate to not live like this anymore. I know now what is meant by the saying: *'You have to get sick and tired of being sick and tired if things are going to change in your life.'* I had reached that point.

While Mike was away, I made my move. I rushed and packed my belongings, then I got the girls out of school and packed their belongings. I had a short window of time. However, as I mentioned earlier, sometimes unexpected things

Finally Free

happen, so stay calm. Mike unexpectedly came home while I was packing my things. Of all the times, he decided to come home early on this day. He walked through the door and saw what I was doing, but I stayed calm. Sure, I was nervous and scared, but I simply played it off like I wasn't and continued to do what I was doing. Mike didn't say anything either. He took a moment and took it all in, realizing that I was about to leave him. At that moment, he walked over to me, and with a balled up fist, punched me so hard in the ribs I could barely breathe. I fell over a chair and hit the floor, writhing in pain, and gasping for air. Tears were streaming down my cheeks. Mike stood stone-faced, his eyes stern and piercing as if to say 'I hate you too.' I suppose that was his going away gift. He then turned and walked away without saying a word while I laid on the floor.

I just laid on the ground in intense pain, wondering what Mike would do next. Was he going to come back and finish me off? Was he going to stomp on me again like he'd done many times before? I didn't know what to expect. Just then, I heard the shower running. I raised myself up with one hand; the other hand on my ribs while I struggled to lift myself. Once on my feet, I ran and got my bags, rounded up the girls, and we got up out of that apartment faster than you can bat an eye. We moved into a shelter and prepared to start a new life.

I had to return to work the next day since I couldn't afford to lose my job. I asked a co-worker that I trusted to run an x-ray on my ribs since they were hurting so bad. She ran the x-ray. Afterward, she informed me that I had a set of cracked ribs. I asked her not to tell the doctor, but to keep this between us, which she did. She looked out for me.

Chapter 7: The Devil Always Comes Back

I DON'T SEE NOTHING WRONG WITH A LITTLE BUMP AND GRIND

My girls and I had our own living space at the shelter. Thank God! No Mike around! Hallelujah! We quickly made some friends with a few of the residences, which helped us in the transition phase. Although I was still in pain due to my ribs being fractured, I had to continue to work through the pain. I carried on at the doctor's office as if I was okay. Also, I was able to get a ticket to the R. Kelly concert, which I planned to attend. Out of all of the hell I'd gone through, I needed it.

At the shelter, there was a curfew for the residences. The facilitators let me stay out late for the concert. There I was, a grown woman living with a curfew, asking permission to stay out past a certain hour like I was a child; this was a small price to pay for the choices I made in life. After receiving the clearance, I was off to the James L. Knight Center for the concert. The place was packed with thousands of people. I was there with a short dress and stilettos on, ready to relax, unwind, and let the sweet sounds of *I Don't See Nothing Wrong* and *Step In The Name of Love* wash over me like a cool breeze on a hot summer's day; this would be my freedom party. Suddenly, someone called my name.

"Ortavia!" When I looked back, I saw it was my cousin and his wife. How they were able to spot me out of all of those people is a mystery, but they did. We talked for a little bit. I decided to wait around with them for a few just in case they were going to get into something after the show, then I heard another voice calling out my name.

"Ortavia!" That voice sounded familiar, too familiar. "Ortavia!" They called out a second time. My heart dropped

Finally Free

into my stomach. From the sound of that voice, I knew who it was. It was Mike. Out of all of the places, and out of all of the people around, he managed to find me. I could sense him approaching me from behind. I kept looking straight ahead while walking, speeding up, pretending I didn't hear him calling my name, but he caught up with me. When I turned around, the sight of his face paralyzed me with fear. The last time we stood face to face was when he broke my ribs; I hadn't spoken to him since then. Now, I was standing face to face with him. I felt relieved that so many people surrounded us, knowing he wouldn't attempt to hurt me there.

Rather than keep moving like I should have, I decided to give him my time and attention. We began to talk. His first words were, "You had to put on the shortest thing out here." He was still Mike, a control-freak. I knew I had plenty of time before I had to be back at the shelter, so we lingered around for a little while; and unfortunately, before it was all over, I was back in Mike's bed in West Palm Beach, Florida.

They say, if you give the devil an inch, he'll take a mile. If you hang around and talk to the devil, he'll undoubtedly lure you back into the bondage he once had you in. The best way to deal with him is to ignore him, not give him the time of day, to avoid sitting and talking to him as if you're smarter than him. Satan is much more intelligent than you and I. He's been in the game of deception for thousands of years, and he's successfully brought down entire civilizations and kingdoms (Isaiah 14:12). So what makes you believe you can outsmart him? Once you play his game, you lose. Once you imagine that you can play with fire and not get burned, you end up getting burned alive.

It was no coincidence that out of all of the people at

Chapter 7: The Devil Always Comes Back

that concert, Mike found me; that wasn't chance or happenstance; it was supernaturally orchestrated; it was a set up by the Adversary. Like the Bible says, Satan is like a roaring lion seeking whom he may devour (1 Peter 5:8). Lions will stalk their prey for miles, waiting for the perfect moment to attack. In the same way, the devil will stalk you, following you around from a distance, and wait for a moment of weakness to unveil itself so that he can pounce on you. You may be going strong right now, staying away from that relationship, steering clear of that substance (drug or alcohol), avoiding that vice or addiction, but the Adversary is still hiding in the shadows, lurking, stalking you, waiting for that one moment of weakness to arise so that he can reintroduce you to the very destructive habits, vices, and additions you fought tooth and nail to get away from. Someone may say or do something that upsets you and rattles your nerves, prompting you to run back to that vice or addiction for relief. Some stressful situation may catch you off guard, causing you to look for solace in that toxic relationship. The difficulty of paying bills on your own may cause you to entertain the idea of going back to that abusive environment for a false sense of security. I don't know what it is that you may be trying to escape, but I do know that if you don't shut the door the devil keeps using to enter into your life through you'll always remain trapped.

    Mike knew what to say to me to get me back into his bed because he knew what my weaknesses were. My self-esteem was low; and my heart, which was battered and bruised not only due to Mike, but from the previous men I'd become attached to, was easy prey for abusers. Allowing myself to get damaged initially may not have been my choice, but refusing to get healed was my choice.

My door was open to the enemy. A poor self-image, a desire to please people, poor self-esteem, negative self-talk, and unforgiveness towards myself and others kept me going back to a destructive bed for a moment of temporary bliss that was always sweet in the beginning but sour in the end. That's the lure of sin; it is always exciting and fun in the beginning, but the "end thereof is death" (Proverbs 14:12). God desires that we walk in longterm healing, not a temporary fix to a deep problem. Sex is a band-aid placed over a broken heart. Alcohol and drugs are just band-aids placed over wounded emotions. If your arm is falling off, you don't go and look for a band-aid. You go to the hospital, to the Emergency Room. With that being in mind, temporary pleasure (or reverting to that comfortable coping mechanism) isn't going to solve the real problem; instead, it's going to prevent you from getting healed and set free by keeping you distracted. We must break the addiction to pleasure! Then, and only then can we find true healing and deliverance.

You can run to a new location, skip town and relocate to a new city, or a new state, even a new country; better yet, you can relocate to a new planet, but guess what, the devil will still show up there and attempt to lure you back into bondage, and he will be successful in doing so. Why? It's because you can escape every place but one place, yourself. You can't escape *you*. Wherever you go, you take *you* with you. So, if your negative thinking and sinful nature is the real problem, those things will always give the enemy an entryway into your life wherever you may be. That's what I couldn't understand. I couldn't understand how Mike found me amidst a sea of people in a crowded venue, and how I so

Chapter 7: The Devil Always Comes Back

quickly ended up back in his bed. It wasn't him; it was me. I had to get free from within so that I could finally break the cycle of returning to my vomit.

> "And when people escape from the wickedness of the world by knowing our Lord and Savior Jesus Christ and then get tangled up and enslaved by sin again, they are worse off than before. It would be better if they had never known the way to righteousness than to know it and then reject the command they were given to live a holy life. They prove the truth of this proverb: 'A dog returns to its vomit.' And another says, 'A washed pig returns to the mud.'" (2 Peter 2:20-22, NLT)

Like a dog, I returned to my own self-destructive behavior. I left the shelter and went right back to Mike. It was back to the vomit, back to the mud. It was back to the beatings, the cursing, the belittling and berating, the mistreatment, and neglect; but this time, an older demon showed up, one that I thought I'd escaped but didn't.

Finally Free
Points To Remember

- Don't try to be smart; instead, apply God's wisdom to every situation. Wisdom is following God's instructions. When God says leave, then leave! Don't try to be cunning and come up with your own plan.
- Have an "Exit Plan" when looking to escape an abusive relationships. Be sure to call a domestic abuse hotline (I've listed a few in the back of this book) and inform them of your situation so that they can guide you in creating an exit strategy.

CHAPTER 8
OUT OF CONTROL

THIS TIME WHEN I RETURNED, A FEW THINGS HAD changed. First, we moved from the apartment and into a rental house. Secondly, two more of Mike's children came to live with us. Now it was a party of eight. But not everything changed. Mike hadn't changed. Just like before, I ended up doing all of the work while Mike continued to Mike play around. I was working two jobs, going to the kids' after-school and church activities (one of my daughters was a drum major in the band at her junior high school), and doing all of the household chores. I kept the kids busy in school and church, and I stayed busy with work and church, dancing on the church dance team, which was therapeutic. I'd forget about the world while dancing. Mike stayed high most of the time, and he started to spiral out of control with a gambling addiction. He'd grown worse since the last time we were together, and the level of violence was about to go to another level.

Finally Free

One day, while at work, Mike called the office rambling on a bunch of nonsense. He sounded like he was high. He was saying things like he hated coming home to me and the kids high. I didn't want to entertain his mess, so I hung up on him. Afterward, he called back, this time sounding even more erratic. He started demanding that I come home, to which I replied no. He demanded again that I leave work and go home, but I explained to him that I couldn't leave because I didn't have anyone else to cover for me. That only incensed him. He threatened to come to my job and "start shooting" if I didn't do what he said. I told my co-worker to hide, quick. I revealed to her that my crazy boyfriend was on his way up there with a gun. The office was deep in the cut, away from the main road, out of sight, which heightened my concern. When Mike arrived, he jumped out of the car and stormed towards the front door. He looked like he hadn't slept any the night before. While there, I lied and told him I was waiting for another girl to come and relieve me. He waited around for a few minutes before finally deciding to leave. After he left, my co-worker and I were relieved. I was embarrassed, though. Thankfully, she didn't report the incident to the boss or the police.

After leaving the office, Mike called back two more times to see if my replacement had arrived. I told him she hadn't arrived yet. After that, he stopped calling. Later that evening, when I got home, I found him sound asleep. Maybe his behavior was due to him being high; but even if that was the case, it still didn't excuse what he did.

A GENERATIONAL CURSE

My oldest daughter was beginning to act differently around

Chapter 8: Out Of Control

the house. As a mother, I could sense when something was off with my kids, and something was off. One night, while Mike was gambling at the gambling house, he overheard two older men talking about these two girls they had been hooking up with. He was shocked when one of the girls mentioned was my oldest daughter. Mike immediately called me to tell me what happened. I couldn't believe what I was hearing.

My oldest daughter had been acting more detached and distant lately. She didn't seem to have an interest in school anymore, nor in any of the extracurricular activities she was involved in at school. Her mind wasn't remotely in-tune with the activities at the church. I didn't know what she was doing at that point. What I did know was she had started to skip school. Where was she going? What was she doing and who was she doing it with? I was determined to find out. Mike gave me a piece of the puzzle. I discovered she was living promiscuously, sleeping around with older men. Whether or not she was doing it for money, I didn't know, but she was beginning to live dangerously.

I didn't know why my oldest daughter was sleeping around with older men. She wouldn't talk to me, but she did talk to my sister, and what I learned from my sister hit me like a Mike Tyson punch to the gut.

I confronted my oldest daughter that night about what I heard. She denied everything. The next day, she got up to go to school, but she never went to school; instead, she ran away. Before running away, she stopped by my sister's house and shared with her the reason why she was running away; and although my sister and I were still on bad speaking terms, she did share with me what my daughter told her. My daughter told her that Mike raped her. The news hit me hard because I was raped and molested as a child. I never shared that with my daughters. I never really shared that with anyone. I hid that fact. Following my rape, I experienced shame. I was ashamed of myself and my body. I felt dirty and powerless.

People who experience molestation and rape usually find themselves harboring negative thoughts and emotions towards themselves. They may believe they were directly responsible for the violation as if they asked for it or invited it; they also feel powerless and weak because they were unable to stop it from happening. The act of rape robs the victim of a sense of power, and this powerlessness takes a negative toll on one's self-esteem. When feeling guilty over the rape, we'll further punish ourselves with other self-destructive behaviors such as cutting, drugs, alcohol, and promiscuity. They lose their sense of value and allow themselves to continually be abused sexually by predators, thinking they deserve to be mistreated and misused. This was a source of my problems; it was that hidden factor that shaped many of the negative feelings I harbored towards myself. Also, because I tried to suppress that event, much of the damaging effects of that event controlled me unconsciously. I was battling this demon long before I met Mike. When Mike came into my life, I was already beaten down; he just took care of the leftovers.

Researchers and mental health experts describe the effects of sexual assault on survivors in numerous articles. Common symptoms that are listed are depression, post-traumatic stress disorder, self-harm, suicidal thoughts, eating disorders, sleep disorders, low self-esteem, anger, sexually deviant behavior (such as promiscuity and commitment issues), maladjustment in school, self-mutilation, and

Chapter 8: Out Of Control

dating victimization and abuse. Many of these symptoms I experienced as a child without realizing it. We might attempt to dismiss these signs in our lives, claiming they're simply phases we will eventually grow out of, but that's not true. Unconsciously, I gravitated towards victimization and abuse, especially in my adult years. That explained a lot; it revealed to me why I insisted on remaining in a toxic relationship characterized by abuse, and why I preferred to play the victim rather than take control of my life. Victimization is about self-pity, and self-pity helps to minimize the emotional pain we feel when subjected to painful experiences. I had to decide whether to stay a victim or get free. Choosing freedom means you stop saying "poor me" and start taking back the power over your own life, and this also means you become entirely responsible for the actions and decisions and consequences you face in your own life. You can no longer blame anyone else for the things you do—it's all on you.

    I was raped as a child. My sister claimed my daughter said she was raped, although she denied it when I confronted her about the claim. I kept my rape a secret. Secrets destroy us from within. Silence kills us slowly. Being confronted with my daughter's sudden actions and her *secret* caused me to revisit that which had been eating away at my soul for years like cancer. Believe it or not, I believe this was a part of God's plan to rescue me. I was being forced to face a demon from my past, one that I thought was dead and buried. You can't defeat the issues of your past by ignoring them. Whatever you choose to ignore will grow behind the scenes until finally gaining enough power to control your life.

    I was watching a generational curse develop right before my eyes. All of this was a set-up to get my daughter(s) to walk down the same path that I chose to go down. Satan planned to guide my girls in the same direction as he did me so that they could experience a life of physical abuse, never valuing themselves and recognizing their significance and worth. Moreover, his ultimate goal for them would be to overwhelm and smother them emotionally to the point of suicide. That's his goal for all of us truthfully. He wants all of us to miss our God-given purposes, overlook our God-given potentials, live unfilled lives; attempt to fill our internal voids with drugs, alcohol, promiscuous sex, and other vices; and then die before our times, only to end up in a burning hell for all of eternity.

When my daughter ran away, I called the cops and reported her missing. Both Mike and I were surprised by her actions and the revelations that were coming out about her. Perhaps she made up the rape allegation as a way of diverting the attention away from her and placing it on Mike after the revelation of her promiscuous activities came to light. It seemed that way. In either case, I was weighed down with a ton of stress to the point that I couldn't sleep. I could barely eat; neither could I concentrate. I was in a place of torment.

GOD'S FINAL WARNING

Due to the stress I was under, I thought I was about to have a nervous breakdown. What gave me the strength during this season was tuning in to the television before heading off to work and seeing this young preacher on there by the name of Jamal Bryant. It was the words he said in his sermon that resonated with me:

"You will not die in this! It was designed to break

Chapter 8: Out Of Control

you, but your answer is here now!"

Yes, everything I was dealing with was designed to break me. Mike tried to break me, my past was designed to break me, and that rape was designed to break me, but I'm still standing. After realizing this, I got my fight back.

I continued to listen to that young preacher as he hammered the point home. I let the television blast throughout the house that morning. God was speaking a life-changing word. After this experience, I began to pursue God with a greater force. I was hungrier than ever for His presence. I was starting to hear Him a lot clearer. I began to increase in my study of the Bible and in my prayer time. My prayer was for God to draw me closer to Him, to forgive me for my sins, and shape me into the woman He wanted me to be. I wanted Him more than I desired my sin. I recognized that I needed Him more than I needed Mike and anyone else. Like God says in His Word, "Come close to God, and God will come close to you" (James 4:8, NLT).

One Sunday morning during service, the power of God was in the building real strong. Under the anointing, the pastor of the church began to prophesy. I was already crying like a baby while being touched by the power of God, but now God was about to get my attention even more. The pastor boldly declared, "There is someone in this place that is in a domestic relationship, and if you don't get out now you will die!" My heart told me he was talking about me. The Holy Spirit had given him a word of knowledge concerning my situation, but pride kicked in. A part of me wanted to hold on to the facade that I was powerful, in control, and happy. Pride makes us hide our sins and real conditions and pretend to be okay when we're not. Pride is the biggest hindrance to our healing, deliverance, and breakthrough. That's also why pride is the sin that got Lucifer kicked out of God's heavenly kingdom.

Because of my pride, I didn't step forward that Sunday. I didn't want to expose the fact that I was experiencing a living hell all while presenting to the congregation this image of a strong, happy woman who had everything together. I didn't want to taint that beautiful image. Sure, there was turmoil taking place in my personal life, and much dirt had gotten out about Mike and me to our family due to the recent developments, but not everyone knew what was going on. I still tried to maintain an image, at least in the church; but God didn't quit on me. He called my name again the following week during Sunday service. That Sunday, the pastor got up and repeated it: "Someone in here is in a domestic relationship, and if you don't get out you will die!" Then he added, "My wife and I will be waiting after church at the pulpit. Come." *This is serious. This is the second time God warned me*, I thought. *I can't let my pride get in the way of my healing, deliverance, and breakthrough. This time, I didn't care if anyone was looking at me.* I had to step forward. I went down and spoke with the pastor after church. He and the first lady talked with me for a few minutes and then prayed with me. The first lady then set up an appointment for the two of us to meet privately that Tuesday. During our meeting, one of the first questions the first lady asked me was, "Why didn't you just call the police?"

"It's not that easy when you're being threatened all of the time," I responded. "You don't understand. It looks easy from the outside looking in." I had an excuse to cover every

Chapter 8: Out Of Control

one of my actions. However, after our meeting, much of the discussion weighed heavily on my mind; and furthermore, the Word of God began to convict me of my sin (of fornication). Mike and I were not married; therefore, we didn't belong in the bed together. We weren't supposed to be playing house, so I started sleeping on the couch each night.

SHOTS FIRED!

Over time, the tension between Mike and I started to reach a fever pitch. It got really hot when one of his lovers showed up at our house in broad daylight. That day, I was driving his truck home from work when I noticed a vehicle was trailing me. I'm street smarts, so I slowed down some to observe the car following me. Everywhere I turned, they turned. When I pulled into my driveway, the car was still behind me. It startled me to see Mike standing in the driveway when I pulled up. He asked me to leave the truck running because he had to go somewhere. Right then, the person in the car hollered from their window at Mike, "I thought you don't fuck with her?" I couldn't believe this chic was crazy enough to follow me to my house. I got out of the truck, ready to go after her when Mike came and restrained me; but I also wanted to kill him. He began to call for my daughter to come outside to get me so that he could get in the truck and drive off. After he left, I hopped into my car and drove off, not caring about the fact that the car didn't even have a tag on it. I was so angry I couldn't think straight. It was time to pick my daughter up from school—she had just gotten back from her trip with the school band. After picking her up, I began heading back home. On my way to the house, I noticed Mike's truck was parked at another house. At that point, I was angry enough

Finally Free

to shoot him, and he realized that too; this had him nervous and acting paranoid. I parked my car on the side of the road and then went up to the house and knocked on the door, but no one answered. I got the sense that Mike knew I was at the door and that spelled bad news for him and the other woman he was with; but I wasn't done with him, so I then went to his truck and set off the alarm, hoping he'd come outside to stop it so that I could light him up. Yes, I was ready to put a bullet in him. He didn't come outside; instead, he called a friend of his and asked them to come and get his truck while he escaped through the back door.

When I arrived at my house, I called my brother and asked him to come over and change the locks at the house, which he did. Later that night, Mike came home and discovered that the locks had been changed. To me, it was a bold move on his part to think that it was okay for him to show up at the house after all he just did. *Forget the dog house; find a hotel; or better yet, you better call Tyrone.* Still, he wasn't going anywhere. It was a scene that night, a spectacle for the entire neighborhood to behold—plenty of shouting, bamming on the door, cursing, and more. I was yelling at him, telling him to leave, feeling disgusted that he would disrespect me in my own house with another woman. Still, he wanted in. He was banging on the door and yelling at me to open the door. He kicked the bottom half of the door in and was trying to crawl through it with a gun in his hand, so I ran and called the cops. Mike then jumped in his vehicle and took off. I notified the landlord of what had occurred. When the police arrived, I told them what happened. The neighbors were staring out of their windows and peeping through their doors; some of them were watching from their yards.

Chapter 8: Out Of Control

The police officer told me that I needed to leave that house. I asked him why should I leave, and he went to the trunk of his car, retrieved a body bag, and then showed it to me and said,

"I don't want to have to come back and put you in it." I was upset by that.

"What makes you think he won't be the one being put in that body bag?" I asked. When I said that, I looked up and saw Mike standing at the top of the street watching everything; he was standing in another neighbor's yard. After the officer left, my brother and the maintenance man working for the landlord came over. They had to fix the door that Mike destroyed trying to get in. I asked my brother to take my girls on with him, feeling afraid to have them around that chaotic environment. I felt like things were going to go down that night. I had my pistol cocked and loaded. A few of my neighbors came over, which was comforting, but I was ready for whatever that night.

About a week later, I was at home with the girls and we were all in the living room. I had been sleeping on the couch in the living room every since that Sunday when God convicted me. I was about to go to sleep on the couch as I usually did when all of a sudden, I felt a vexation in my spirit. *Something* told me not to sleep on the couch that night. A sense of dread came over me. I immediately got up, rounded up the girls, and we went into another room of the house to sleep. At about five o'clock in the morning, I heard gunshots outside of the house. I jumped up quickly and hollered to the girls, "GET DOWN!" While on the floor, I waited a few seconds before checking to see what was going on. Just then, I heard a car speed off just outside the house. After the vehi-

Finally Free

cle sped off, I got up and peeped through the window to see if anyone was outside. I didn't see anyone.

Later that morning, I walked my children to the bus stop for school. When I returned to the house, I noticed several 9 Millimeter bullet casings laying on the ground right in front of the house. When I turned and looked at the house, I noticed nine bullet holes in the wall where the living room sits. Chills shot up and down my spine when I saw that. The spot where the bullets penetrated was the same spot I would have been laying in had I not heeded the warning the Holy Spirit gave me that night. That was terrifying, and yet, reassuring. *Last night would have been a homicide, but God...*

As expected, Mike denied having anything to do with it, but I knew better. A neighbor later identified the vehicle that was parked in front of my house when those shots were fired; the description is the same as Mike's vehicle; even still, Mike denied everything. I wasn't going to wait around until Mike finally finished me off. It was time to move. I informed the pastor and the first lady about what happened, and they sent over a couple of deacons to help me move out of that house and into an apartment I found.

I began rebuilding my life. I got a new job working at a dealership even though I was still working at the hair salon on weekends. I was now more active in the church than ever before—still dancing with the dance ministry. One Sunday, we had to dance to Marvin Sapp's hit song *Never Would Have Made It*. While dancing, the lyrics to the song brought me to tears:

I'm stronger.
I'm wiser.

Chapter 8: Out Of Control

I'm better, so much better.
When I look back over all you brought me through,
I can see that you were the one I held on to...

That song moved me because it was my life's story. I knew I wouldn't have made it without God's protection. I wouldn't have survived the many days and nights of abuse I suffered. I would be dead had God not instructed me to go into a different room *that night*. I wouldn't have survived that suicide attempt. *I never would have made it ... without you, Lord.*

Finally Free

Points To Remember

- Lookout for subtle changes in your child's/children's behavior. If they're acting angry, engaging in reckless and destructive behaviors, acting withdrawn, and other signs of distress and depression, then get to them early before they completely drift away from you.
- Open up to someone about the traumatic experiences you've encountered: things like rape, molestation, abuse, neglect, shame, and other negative experiences. The more you open up and talk about them to others, the more power you gain over them. Find a good counselor or a pastor and open up to them.
- Heed God's warning. When you see that things are getting worst, get out of there. Don't hang around and get yourself killed. If someone threatens to kill you, don't take that lightly.
- Remember: This is a spiritual battle. Developing a generational curse in your family is Satan's goal. He wants to trick your children into repeating your same mistakes. Get free through the power of God so that you can establish a new example and a pattern of generational blessings.

CHAPTER 9
FREE AT LAST

THE WORDS OF THE PREACHER WERE SPOT-ON. If I didn't leave that relationship, I was going to die. I know that now, especially looking back in hindsight. It went from beatings and threats of murder to Mike acting on those threats. He just tried to shoot me; but as strange as it may sound, as much as I despised him, I couldn't get Mike out of my system. I couldn't get away from him, mentally and emotionally. It's easy to divorce someone in your mind, but it's much harder to divorce someone in your heart, especially when you're close intimately. That was my problem. I knew what I needed to do, but struggled with it; this was a struggle between the flesh and the spirit.

I kept God's warning on the forefront of my mind even as I wrestled with the urge to pick up the phone and call Mike. We were now on and off. I was in and out of his bed. The crazy thing is, the more I despised him, the more I couldn't resist being around him. We were now more toxic than we'd ever been. The fights between us now didn't merely involve fists; they now involved weapons. If we didn't separate from one another, someone was going to get killed. It would either be him of me.

Again, I found myself in the position where I was ready to kill Mike; it involved one of his crazy baby mommas who had the audacity to pick up the phone and call me while I was at work. She called to tell me to "stay the hell away from Mike." She then began mentioning personal things about me that no one else would have known unless Mike told them. She even mentioned the time when Mike broke my ribs. *Oh, hell no! She done crossed a line now!* Thank God, my daughter was eavesdropping on my conversation, for had she not jumped in the car when I went head-hunting and intervened when I caught up with Mike, he'd probably be dead and I'd be in prison.

I arrived at Mike's house and parked at an angle where I could remain hidden. Mike hadn't made it home yet, but he was on his way. I soon spotted him, along with one of his friends and his cousin, walking towards his apartment. They also spotted me and then ran. They ran into the apartment and locked the door while trying to keep me out. They saw the big, huge knife I had in my hand. I busted out the window next to the door and let myself in. My daughter, who stole a ride with me, rushed out of the car to intervene. For the first time in my life, I saw real fear in Mike's eyes. To him, I must have looked like a deranged psychopath with a knife looking to gut someone. His baby momma, who, at the time, was standing by the trunk of her car, nearly jumped in the trunk when she saw me coming. She was crying and begging me to leave, and so was Mike's cousin. Mike, however,

Chapter 9: Free At Last

just stood there, frozen with fear. Right then, my daughter hollered out, "Momma, he's not worth it!" She became the voice of reason, causing me to think about what I was about to throw my life away over. *No, Mike isn't worth it*, I thought to myself.

Before that, I was full of rage. Later, the thought of what I'd become frightened me. I had the same look in my eyes that Mike would have when in a fit of rage. If there's one thing I didn't want, it was for me to become consumed with the same hate that consumed Mike; and furthermore, to become the very thing I despised. I know that hatred can only beget hatred. Hate turns us into the very abusers we dread. Even though I'd calmed down by now, I still wanted to leave a message for Mike, so I busted out all of his apartment windows and then proceeded to slash all of the tires on his truck on the way to my car.

Later on, I began to think long and hard about my actions that day. I thought about the look on my daughter's face and wondered what she might have thought when seeing me stand there looking like a crazy woman with a knife. The look in her eyes was sobering. I also thought about what I must have looked like to God; that's when a heavy conviction came over me. *This is not Ortavia. This is not the woman I am called to be.* The devil had a trap set for me at that moment. He wanted me to destroy myself with anger and then lose the future God had for me. I repented to God for the way I acted and what I did.

I was still feeling convicted about what I'd done, so I called Mike's mom and told her about what happened, apologizing for stepping so much out of character. She was understanding and even found it somewhat humorous. My

Finally Free

daughter and I shared a few laughs over that as well. It's funny how when the tables are turned some people can't take what they're so used to dishing out: this time, Mike was the victim, and I was the terror.

That Sunday, I needed to have my mind renewed. I was so happy to be in church. The worship was a life-saver. Right after service, I received a text message from my cousin informing me that there were places for rent in North Carolina for around $300 a month. In the message, she asked me if I was interested in moving, and when. I replied, "Like *yesterday!*" I wanted to get as far away from the drama as I could. A few seconds later, my cousin called. When I answered, I couldn't hold back my tears. I was desperate to get away, desperate for help. Hearing me sob, she gave the phone to her mother. I began sharing with her everything I'd gone through over that past couple of months. Although the property wouldn't be ready for a month, she pulled some strings to get me into a new place as soon as possible.

"Let me call you back," she said. A few minutes later, she called back with some good news. "I have a missionary friend up here. I asked her if she wouldn't mind if you came up there with her to stay, and she said yes." I indicated that I was happy to accept her offer and thanked her for her help. She then gave me the train and the person's contact information. Without informing anyone, I packed my bags and moved to North Carolina, even leaving my daughters behind with my auntie for a month, just so that they could finish the rest of the school year. Once school was out, they later joined me in my new home. It was time for me to start a new life.

Chapter 9: Free At Last

MY NEW LIFE

When I arrived in North Carolina, I immediately went job hunting. I didn't need anything big; I wasn't looking for a corporate office in a high-rise in the middle of the city. I was willing to take whatever I could. I remember going to Burger King and handing them my resume. I got a call back from them the same day telling me I was hired for the Assistant Manager position, but that I needed to start as a cashier for training. Things were shaping up for me. I was blessed with a car to get around in. The greatest part of this experience was that it put a lot of distance between Mike and myself, and it gave me a lot of time to be alone with God. Many of the distractions I faced back home weren't there. I had plenty of time to pray and to reflect. Now, I did call Mike while there, and he was furious over the fact that I'd moved so far away, but that didn't bother me now. To a degree, it tickled me to see him so angry. Now, he was moping like a big baby.

I began experiencing God's presence more, and even having prophetic dreams. This time allowed me to grow spiritually. God knew I needed it, which is why He opened the door for me to leave Florida. As I matured spiritually, He began to speak to me about the deeper issues of the heart, the things that kept me bound throughout my life. One of the issues God spoke to me about was soul-ties. I needed to sever the spiritual connection to Mike. It wasn't enough to put physical distance between us; there had to be a spiritual separation.

What is a soul-tie? It is a spiritual bond two individuals develop when they become sexually active. The Bible explains that anytime you have sex with someone, your soul becomes one with theirs. In 1 Corinthians 6:16, the Apostle

Finally Free

Paul wrote,

> "Do you not know that he who unites himself with a prostitute is one with her in body? For it is said, 'The two will become one flesh.'"

This is also covered in Leviticus chapter eighteen.

My new life couldn't start until I broke the spiritual union I had with Mike; if I didn't, I'd be bound to that old life no matter where I went. I began to pray and ask God for forgiveness for the sin of fornication. Again, I had to call it what it is: "sin." I couldn't justify anymore the arrangement Mike and I had. I couldn't just gloss over it and white-wash it; I had to acknowledge it and repent of it. I had to pray and ask God to release me from the soul-tie and fill me with His Spirit. I had to commit to putting my heart and trust back in God. When I did this, there was no supernatural display that occurred before my eyes—the sky didn't open up, a chorus of angels didn't appear and sing *Hallelujah* or anything like that; but, by faith, a change did occur, and the soul tie was *almost* broken—almost! I say this because there was another step in the process I needed to take, which I'll explain in a moment.

The process of healing had begun, but God was far from through. There were a few more things He needed to deal with in my heart, some soul-wounds that needed to be healed—the journey towards healing started with an unexpected tragedy.

FAMILY TRAGEDY

I received a call from my brother stating that he had cancer

Chapter 9: Free At Last

and was being treated at the hospital. He was about to have surgery. He mentioned that he might not make it off the operating table. That floored me. I was at work when I got the call. All I could do was fall on my knees in the middle of that Burger King and pray. I then hurried up and left work, got the girls, and we drove all night to get back home so I could be by my brother's side. He was shocked to see us and delighted when my daughters sang for him *Spirit* by Luther Barnes. I stayed by his side the entire night, praying for him and believing God for his healing. While I was there, I was surprised to see Mike come by my mom's house to show his support. Even though I didn't want to be around him because of his ways, I always felt like he had a good heart.

I had to be back to North Carolina by the next day—I had to get back to work. I stayed in contact with my brother over the telephone, talking to him and encouraging. I began talking to him about God, and I'm happy to say that I led him back to Christ. While on the phone, he rededicated his life to the Lord. That was one of the best feelings I ever had. Whether he lived or died, I was content in knowing his soul was right with God, and he now had a home in Heaven. It was on December 17, 2008, that my brother made the transition from this life to the next; he made that coveted journey through the pearly gates of Heaven and onto those fabulous streets of gold.

Death reminds us of where our priorities should lie. We only have a short amount of time on this earth, and we should not waste it on toxic relationships and meaningless pursuits. This realization impressed upon me deeply while at my brother's funeral. His life went by so fast, and it was taken so unexpectedly. I thought about my life and what it meant, and what I needed to do to make it impactful in this world. *How can I live out my purpose?* That was my question.

THE TEST

While back home, my *flesh* pulled on me again. Although I was a brand new woman living in a brand new town with a brand new job and a brand new life, I still had—and have—the old sin nature. That goes for all of us who are born again. You never lose the desire to sin; you simply gain a greater willingness to please God and exercise mastery over your sinful desires. So, as a Believer in Christ, rather than sin ruling over you, it is ruled by you. That's why Romans chapter six tells us not to "yield" to sin, but rather submit ourselves to Christ to be used by Him as His vessels.

Mike came by to console me during my time of grief. While at my mom's house, he asked if I wanted to get a hotel room together. I agreed, and we ended up getting one. Perhaps, this was for old time's sake. Whatever the case, it was a familiar feeling. While in that room, all of those old senses came rushing back to me. Everything felt familiar, and yet, it didn't. There was a hint of oddness. I tried to settle down and get comfortable. We talked and reminisced. It's interesting that we mainly talked about the good times, but cut out all of the beatings, the broken ribs, the time he tried to shoot me, the many cases of infidelity, and more. It's like the Children of Israel who were ready to return to Egypt after escaping slavery; their focus was on the fish and herbs they were used to getting, and not the cruelty of the taskmasters they had to endure—the beatings, rapes, murders, etc.

In the room, we did most of the things we used to do; but this time, there was one thing we didn't do—

Chapter 9: Free At Last

While in the bed, I couldn't pull myself to *go with the flow* like I normally would. This time, there was a conviction that rested on me so strongly that all I could do was cry. That made Mike very uncomfortable. Usually, I'd be game; I'd be ready to have sex with him even after he'd hit me, throw me into the wall, do bad things to me, and talk to me like I was trash. Back then, I just felt unworthy of respect and took his abuse as a sign of love and affection. This time, things were different. I had been liberated, and I finally realized it. Spiritually, the connection between us wasn't as strong. My flesh was old, but my spirit was brand new. My heart and love for God much more than my flesh could take.

I just laid in the bed and cried with my back turned towards Mike. He lied there, watching me break down emotionally, silently observed me as if looking at a total stranger. He could sense that there was a change in me. Eventually, we fell asleep with our backs turned towards one another. In the morning, I felt a sense of power I hadn't felt in years; it was a renewed sense of control; this was taken away from me throughout the years. I had been stripped of it through acts such as rape, molestation, rejection, mental, emotional, and physical abuse. I didn't even think I'd ever get it back at one point, but there it was. Each day I said no to sin and the flesh, and the old urges and temptations, the stronger and more confident I became. I was beginning to feel like the old Ortavia again, the one I thought I lost forever.

There was more healing to come. While back home, I spent time with my family. My mother and I spent time bonding and releasing the negativity of the past. I shared with her many of the things I went through but kept secret. A huge part of our healing and deliverance is disclosure. You have to open up about the things you've buried in your heart if you want to regain power over your life. Fear causes us to keep secrets and hide the truth about ourselves; therefore, overcoming fear is the key. God provided both the means and the opportunities for me to reconcile relationships and face the things I was trying to avoid in my life; and in doing so, I never felt more liberated. As I began to talk about the things that were difficult to talk about, I became free from the prison cell of fear that had kept me bound for so long.

God was still uncovering the hidden wounds in my heart. One day, Mike called me with a sense of urgency. He needed me. Previously, I felt raw over the things he put me through; the memories burned in my mind; but now, God was teaching me what it means to walk in His love. I had to muster up every ounce of forgiveness in me to face him and not hold it against him for the cruelty he inflicted on me during our time together. God will put you in a position to bless those that hurt you, help those that hindered you, pray for those that preyed on you, and show love to those that showed you nothing but hatred. That's a real test. My heart was changed. I could stand by his side during a trying season in his life and no longer be affected by the past.

Jesus said in Matthew chapter six that if we only love those who love us back, then our love is not good enough in the sight of God. If we only do good for people we like, then are we are no better than the Pharisees and the hypocrites. It's easy to do good for people you like, those who do good things for you, but the test is when you have to reopen old wounds and revisit faces you've tried to avoid and deal with emotions you tried to suppress. God put me in the position where I had to face all of these things and acknowledge the

Chapter 9: Free At Last

pain I still felt in my heart; and the way I brought closure to that chapter and overcame the pain was not by hiding and dodging it, but by acknowledging it and then counteracting it with a selfless act of love. I had to do good for someone I felt did me wrong. That's why Jesus told us the key to overcoming the evil others do to us is to love and bless them, to counteract their evil deeds with our good deeds. In doing so, we defeat the evil and bitterness inside of us.

I was facing every demon from my past with the help of God; and for every demon that I confronted and conquered, I took back more control over my life that had been stolen. I felt unstoppable like there was nothing that could hold me down. I was on a forgiveness campaign. I forgave everyone: myself, Mike, my ex-husband, ex-boyfriend, those who hurt me as a little girl, my sister, those who rejected me and wounded my heart deeply, and those who dragged my name through the mud while I was going through a private hell. Alongside forgiving myself and others, I started to view myself in a different light: the way God sees me.

MY COMEBACK

I remained with my family for Christmas, but I returned to North Carolina for New Years. In North Carolina, life began to take on a whole new meaning for me. My girls started to excel in school and sports again. They were back active in the church—I found a good church and became active in it. I danced on their dance ministry team. In my personal life, things began to flourish. It's like I escaped a long, dark, cold winter season in my life and entered into spring. Everything began to turn around.

I was blessed to start my own business, a hair salon,

Finally Free

which has been pretty rewarding financially. I also became a grandmother. I couldn't have imagined seeing this day while living in darkness. I didn't even think I'd live long enough to see that day. I thought I would have lost my mind or my life before then. Now, I was looking a precious little gift in the eyes and holding it in my arms. Thankfully, I was now armed with the wisdom to guide those coming after me. Looking into those precious little eyes, all I could think was I would never allow anyone to hurt this little one. I know the world, the cruelty that exists within it, the predators waiting to devour any glimpse of innocence that emerges within it, but that's why God allowed me to survive hell so that I could light the way for those whose paths I come across.

Never did I expect to become a guide and a coach for one of my daughters who had fallen into the cycle of abuse. She was bright, intelligent, and smart like me, but she chose to hook up with the wrong type of man. She had graduated Valedictorian from her school, but the principal wouldn't allow her to speak at the graduation ceremony for good reason. First, she'd been injured and hospitalized after her boyfriend struck her in the eye with the butt of his gun. The worst part is she'd received national acclaim for a project she did on domestic violence; it received coverage by the press and media. It would have been an embarrassment for the Valedictorian of a school who created an award-winning project on domestic violence to be revealed as currently residing in a physically abusive relationship.

At the time, I had already relocated back to Florida. The principal put my daughter on a train and sent her back to Florida after she was released from the hospital. Once she got back to Florida, I carried her home. Before that, she'd

Chapter 9: Free At Last

been living with a guy who was doing the same thing to her that Mike did to me, and she was handling the situation the same way I handled mine. She wanted to be silent and sweep everything under the rug—that's what she saw me do for so long. That was the example that I set for her. I started to feel bad for leaving such an example for my daughter to follow, but then God reminded me that I had been forgiven and that was the past; furthermore, He spoke to my heart to trust Him with my daughter. All I could do was be there for my daughter as a resource and source of support, but it was her choice to follow wisdom or make stupid decisions. She saw the change in me and knew enough about the dangers of domestic violence to know what to do. I provided a new example for her to follow; and now, the choice was hers. I realized that no one is perfect, that every parent will have flaws; I was no different. The Word of God spoke to me from Ezekiel 18:2-4,

> "Why do you quote this proverb concerning the land of Israel: 'The parents have eaten sour grapes, but their children's mouths pucker at the taste'? As surely as I live, says the Sovereign Lord, you will not quote this proverb anymore in Israel. For all people are mine to judge—both parents and children alike. And this is my rule: The person who sins is the one who will die."

As parents, we sometimes set bad examples, but when God corrects us and we, in turn, correct our sons and daughters, it is up to them to decide what type of life they want to live. We can't keep feeling guilty about their actions, especially once they've seen God transform our lives. Forgive yourself and pray for your child or loved one. Be there for them, having arms opened wide, ready to embrace them, but let them make their own decisions. That is the only thing you can do.

THE FINAL STEP IN MY DELIVERANCE

One day, out of the blue, my phone rang. When I answered it, I was shocked to hear *his* voice again. It was Mike. *How did he get my number?* I wondered. I was upset over him tracking me down and calling me. I started to let him have it over the phone, but then he said something that made me pause in my tracks; he uttered the three magic words I'd secretly been wanting to hear from him: "I am sorry." When he expressed remorse over the way he'd treated me, a calm fell over me. I was lost for words. He was spewing his heart out, owning up to all of the things he did in our relationship. Stunned, all I could think was God must have been working on him pretty strongly. Mike then asked me for forgiveness, not knowing I had already forgiven him in my heart; but despite having already done it in my heart, I needed to tell him I forgave him, which I did verbally; this was to free him.

When I relocated back to Florida, I moved back into my mother's house. I continued to do hair and was working at a beauty store and going to school at night to become a massage therapist. I was reestablishing myself when, while at church one day, the pastor came and spoke a word of prophecy over me about me being in the ministry. Of course, I was taken aback by that. I was content with being on the dance team at the church. I certainly wasn't expecting that. To discover that the call of God on my life was to preach the Gospel was a big deal; this would be a big leap for me. At first, I

Chapter 9: Free At Last

felt unworthy of the call. *How could God use someone like me, someone with my background, having gone through the things I went through? I made too many mistakes. I have too many shortcomings. I can't say I've made the wisest and best decisions in my life. I've not set the best example for my kids. And I still have a lot of things that I'm dealing with in my personal life while trying to get back on my feet. I'm not in a place where anyone would want to listen to me. God, you have the wrong person.* These and other thoughts flooded my mind; and yet, they didn't deter God and cancel His plan for me. The pastor insisted that I enroll in his ministry training classes in preparation for where God was getting ready to take me and what He was getting ready to do inside of me.

You would think that news like that would be a cause for rejoicing; but for me, it was a source of stress. I was excited and terrified at the same time. I didn't know how to handle this and what to do. God was shaking me out of my comfort zone. Sometimes, when going through stressful situations, we tend to make hasty decisions; mine was to revert to an old habit, which was Satan's plan all the long. I picked up the phone and called Mike and asked him if he wanted to hang out and play pool. Of course, one thing led to another, and before I knew it, I was right back in his bed; but this time, things were so awkward that neither one of us could enjoy the experience. Sex with him felt gross. Even Mike couldn't even get into it. Satan, however, was looking to destroy us before God could finish His work in our lives.

The day after our sexual encounter, Mike called me and asked me if I had given him *something*. He said he went to the bathroom and puss started coming out of his penis. I responded to his accusation, "Boy, you crazy!" However, I

Finally Free

thought about it: *What if he gave me something?* Right then, the scare got real. If he was emitting something, there might have been something wrong with his body. He might have been carrying a disease but didn't know it, or maybe he did know he was infected, but wanted to pin it on me out of guilt. I immediately called my doctor whom I had seen just a couple of days prior before leaving North Carolina—I went there for a checkup where my doctor discovered cancer cells inside of me. My doctor informed me that if Mike had puss coming out of his penis, that meant he was already infected. Also, my Pap test results came back normal, revealing that there was nothing wrong with my body; and yet, I insisted on being seen again so that I could take an HIV test. While awaiting the results of my lab test, all kind of thoughts were going through my mind—*If Mike gave me something, especially HIV, I'm going to murder him. God, forgive me! I hope this isn't happening!* I waited while wondering, hoping, praying, and imaging the worse. Thoughts were racing through my mind at a thousand miles per second. Finally, the doctor contacted me with the results. They were negative. I was so relieved that God gave me another chance. I distinctively heard God speak into my spirit, *I gave you all of the signs not to go through with it (going back to sexual sin), but you still have not died to your flesh, but I have protected you. You shall live and not die.* In my spirit, I realized that this was a warning, a big warning. I was now done with playing games. That was the final scare. I realized at that moment, just how quick it could all be over. It only takes one mistake; just *one*.

    Satan uses sexual sin to trap us and destroy our bodies—and souls. God isn't trying to make our lives miserable when He tells us to come out of fornication (sexual immo-

Chapter 9: Free At Last

rality and sin); He's trying to save our lives. HIV is real. AIDs is real. So many people are dying slowly, and painfully from these diseases today. All it takes is one sexual encounter, and your life is forever over; just one slip-up. So when you hear the Holy Spirit telling you to go in another direction when temptation is staring you in your face, you would be wise to heed His warning and walk away. It's not worth what you're about to lose: your health, reputation, blessings, and life.

I realized that Satan had a hit out on my life. He was still seeking to trap me. I began to meditate on the Word of God intensely, studying 2 Corinthians 5:17, which says,

> "Therefore, if any man be in Christ, he is a new creature, old things have passed away and behold all things are made new."

God made me a brand new woman; therefore, the old Ortavia was dead and buried as the next verse reveals:

> "Therefore, we are buried with Him (Christ Jesus) by baptism into death: that just as Christ was raised up from the dead by the glory of the Father, even so we also should walk in newness of life" (Romans 6:4).

These verses reminded me of who I really am. I'm new; therefore, I'm to live new, act new, walk in newness, and get ready to experience new blessings and breakthroughs. Meditating on those two verses changed my thinking and perspective and put me back on track in my life. They gave me the power to shut the door in the face of the enemy who was trying

Finally Free

to destroy both me and Mike's lives. God was doing a work in Mike the same way He was me, and the flesh was getting in the way. Sexual sin was a hindrance to Mike's deliverance and transformation, and it was the door Satan was using to try to reenter my life. I decided to turn my back on sin and let God do what He needed to do in my life and Mike's life.

I discovered behind this incident that just because you forgive someone, that doesn't mean you have to go back to the things of the past. I'd forgiven Mike, but I wasn't obligated to jump back into a relationship with him, neither were we obligated to get married. Forgive and move on; that was what I needed to do. I couldn't afford to backtrack into the bondage I just came out of. It's okay to part ways with the past, which is what I did. I shut the door of that chapter once and for all.

During my process of deliverance, God began speaking to me again about releasing the past by completing the process of breaking the soul-tie I had with Mike and with other men from my past. He spoke to me prophetically one mid-week service at church about getting rid of certain "objects" that were binding me to the past. The Bible tells us in 2 Corinthians 6:18,

> "Wherefore come out from among them, and be ye separate, saith the Lord, and touch not the unclean thing, and I will receive you…"

It was one thing to stop seeing Mike, but another to gather all of the belongings I'd acquired during my time with Mike and get rid of them; this was the final step in getting free from yesterday. It's like the Bible says in Acts 19:19-20, where

Chapter 9: Free At Last

it describes the Christians in one town who God called to repent of their hidden sin of practicing witchcraft, "A number of them who had been practicing sorcery brought their incantation books and burned them at a public bonfire. The value of the books was several million dollars. So the message of the Lord spread widely and had a powerful effect." Notice that the Word of God and the power of God didn't spread throughout the town until the Christians repented and destroyed their idols (occult books, occult tools, and other tools of divination and witchcraft). Likewise, there might be some things God is telling you to get rid of, burn up, or throw in the trash can. Maybe you need to take *those DVDs* and toss them out; perhaps you need to take those old clothes and trash them. Maybe you need to take that obituary of that former boyfriend and burn it. God might even be telling you to get rid of the ashes of that dead loved one you have sitting on your mantelpiece above the fireplace. Jesus said to one man, "let the dead bury the dead," meaning we're not to obsess over the dead as if we can't live without them. Engaging in such actions can open doors for demonic intrusion into our lives, and these spirits will torment us and attempt to take us back into past bondages.

    I know what the prophet of the Lord told me. I accepted what God was doing in me. It was time for a complete release of yesterday so that I could fully embrace tomorrow. I got all of the items that I had kept from my past, the things that attached me to Mike and every other lover in my history, and I laid everything on the bed—this included pictures, perfumes, jewelry, clothes, and other gifts purchased for me by these men, even items they bought for my girls. I would sleep next to these items in the bed because they comforted

Finally Free

me, reminding me of the 'good ole' days.' These items had become my idols. I felt like I couldn't part ways with them. I'd stare at them, wear them; and turn to them for comfort, pride, and a sense of identity. They were the gateway to yesterday's bondages. That's what idols do: keep you reminded of the past so that you can't focus on the future God has for you. God instructed me to get rid of my idols so that I could finally be free, and I was not about to argue with God. If the Christians in that town could destroy items that were very expensive, with a combined value of several million dollars, then no idol is more valuable than your deliverance.

Once I collected all of those items, I placed them on my bed, and then grabbed a big trash bag and trashed them. After doing this, I felt a supernatural peace my spirit. It was like something had fallen off of me. I felt a supernatural release occur; and that night, I slept more peacefully than ever before. I didn't just engage in a symbolic act; this was a spiritual divorcement from demonic power in my life; and now, I was completely free.

Once free in my spirit, it didn't matter anymore what happened to me; the fear and anxiety that once controlled my life were now gone. I was no longer stressed over my situation. I was dealing with setbacks and financial woes; my car went out, and my daughter dropped out of college, but I was free. My grandson and I were sleeping on the couch, but I didn't feel worried or bad; I was free. I reacted differently to the same struggles I'd experienced before. I had optimism and a level of faith and expectation that was supernatural in nature, and this filled me with a joy I couldn't explain. I had a feeling that everything was going to be all right; and sure enough, everything turned out just fine. God was true

Chapter 9: Free At Last

to His Word. He kept every promise made to me. I got a job in the career field I went to school for, massage therapy. I got my own place. I recovered everything that I lost. I began to experience unexpected blessings from other people God would send into my life. It was amazing! People would sow unexpectedly into me. God blew my mind, but that's not all. On October 24, 2009, I preached my trial sermon entitled *Strengthening Your Faith by Removing The Weight*. I was able to minister this message because I lived it. That was my story.

Today, this can be your story. It's not over. There's so much God desires to do in you. It's time for you to open your eyes and see the bright future that awaits you. It's bright! I can assure you that your best days are ahead of you. There's a peace you never had, a joy you never experienced, a level of confidence you never had, and a freedom you never enjoyed waiting for you. God desires to give this to you. You deserve it. Receive it! It's time for your victory lap. Yes, it is time for your transformation, and your life to be overtaken by God's best.

It's your time to finally be free!

Finally Free

Points To Remember

- Getting free from past sexual partners involves breaking "Soul-ties." To break a soul-tie, you must **repent of the sin of fornication, denounce any attachment with the spirit of the other person(s) you slept with, get rid of items given to you by that person (idols), and seek to be filled with God's Spirit.**
- Remember: We wrestle not against flesh and blood, so domestic violence and fornication (sexual sin and immorality) are demonic assaults on your God-given destiny and purpose in life. This calls for war—spiritual warfare!

THE FINAL WORD

My story is not unique. There are many people—men and women—who've escaped the grip of domestic violence and have gone on to find freedom, peace, happiness, and fulfillment in their lives. Freedom is a choice; it won't come unless you seek it. Even though God had a plan to free me, I had to accept His plan and choose to obey His instructions even when I didn't understand what He was leading me to do.

Your freedom begins with God. Domestic abuse is a demonic attack on your life and health; it is designed to destroy you from within and destroy your family. There are things the devil wants to withhold from you, and for him to do this, he must trick you into giving up on the power and potential you truly have in life. He wants you to feel worthless and trick you into believing you're worthy of disrespect and abuse. He wants to tear you down from within, but I'm here to put an end to Satan's schemes in your life.

If you want to put an end to what the enemy is doing

Finally Free

in your life, start by praying this prayer:

> Lord Jesus, forgive me for my sins. I repent if I've lived in open and deliberate sin and disobedience to you. Lord, I surrender my life to you so that you can lead me, guide me, and make me the person you want me to be.
>
> Lord, I repent for agreeing with the enemy in my life. I am not worthless, useless, ugly, and undesirable. You didn't design for me to be a victim of abuse. Instead, you predestined that I have the best, be treated with respect, be loved, have a great and loving relationship, and live in total freedom. I accept your best for my life. I am who you say I am. I am loved by you, worthy, confident, powerful, and full of greatness.
>
> Today, I forgive everyone that has ever hurt me, and I forgive myself. I harbor no negative feelings towards them nor myself. I thank you God that I am now stronger as a result of my past failures, and not defeated by them. I am wiser, stronger, and more powerful because of them.
>
> Lord, I repent for harboring idols in my life. Any idol, any object or item that allows the enemy access into my life, lead me to it so that I may throw it out of my home and life. I choose to allow you to reign as King in my life. Let my home be a place where your presence dwells.
>
> I surrender my family to you. Have your way in their lives. This day, I choose your will for my life. I thank you that I am free. Today, I am free. In Jesus name, Amen.

After praying that prayer, the next step I want you to take is to contact an emergency hotline. Here are a few hotlines you can call:

- National Domestic Violence Hotline: 1-800-799-SAFE (7233)
- Rape, Abuse, and Incest National Network (RAINN): 1-800-656-HOPE (4673)

Remember: Silence and secrecy allow negative experiences to control your life. Be bold! Be open! Get free by opening your mouth and saying something to someone that can help you today! SPEAK UP!

Lastly, find a good church home where you can grow spiritually and become a part of it. Get involved. Get connected. Also, dedicate time to reading God's Word, the Bible. Start by studying the verses that talk about God's love; also look up the ones that talk about your new identity in Christ. It's crucial that you discover who you are and what God thinks about you. I want you to know that you are very important to God, so spend time getting to know Him and yourself—your *true* self created in the image and likeness of God.

It's your time! Today is your day to get free! Be free!

ABOUT THE AUTHOR

Ortavia Taylor is an entrepreneur, business owner, and Minister of the Gospel. She carries a true heart of compassion and endeavors to help people obtain a sense of wholeness and healing through the transforming Word and power of God. Mentoring, counseling, and praying for others is her true passion.

Ortavia holds several licenses as a CNA/PCT, Cosmetologist, and Massage Therapist. She is also a certified Health and Nutrition Life Coach.

Ortavia is a mother of three beautiful daughters, Ashley, Deshantia, and Raynesha, and a grandmother of five: Jeromiah, Kobe, Kloei, Kali, and Giovanni (her miracle grand-baby). She's an active intercessor for Crystal Pugh Ministries and Soulfood Sessions with Niya.

Currently, she is working on three more books.

To contact author, go to:
www.JustTaylorMade.com
Justtaylormade1@gmail.com
Instagram: JustTaylorMade1
Facebook: Just Taylor Made

Business Contact Number:
(678) 671-1615

www.ingramcontent.com/pod-product-compliance
Lightning Source LLC
Chambersburg PA
CBHW030329080526
44584CB00012B/775